THE ART OF RETIR

D1503764

THE ART OF RETIRING WHOLE

A NON-FINANCIAL GUIDE TO RETIRING WITH PURPOSE,
PRODUCTIVITY AND ENDLESS POSSIBILITIES

Ryan S. Kidd

ISBN-13: 9781523841271
ISBN-10: 1523841273

I dedicate this book to two of my favorite retirees, Ronald Smithson and Roger Kidd.

As I conclude this book, I am filled to capacity with gratitude for two of the greatest retirees and men I have been privileged to know- my dear friend, Ron Smithson, and my dad, Roger Kidd. Both have exemplified what it means to retire whole-with purpose, productivity and passion. Ron, who just passed from this world and into the arms of his Father a mere two days ago had more hobbies than anyone I have ever met. From jewelry making, hunting (really just camping with guns), photography, guitar playing, four wheeling, car restoration and probably his favorite hobby, helping others, he personified living life to its fullest and I am ever grateful for his encouragement and guiding hand in my adult life. My dad, Roger Kidd, has lived his life with a peaceful persistence in always doing the right thing. He showed me what it means to be a dad, husband, and son of God. He is who I look to when I need a nudge in the right direction. He can out-hike, jog, and bike me any day of the week. He gives of his time to help those in need and never complains about anything. He is one of the greatest gifts life has afforded me and he has certainly shown me the formula for retiring whole and so much more.

TABLE OF CONTENTS

INTRODUCTION

THE US GOVERNMENT reports that seventy-five million people will turn sixty-five prior to the year 2033, and the impact is being felt already. Health Services Research reported the following challenges of caring for the elderly in 2030[1]:

- Ensuring that society develops payment and insurance systems for long-term care that work well
- Taking advantage of advances in medicine and behavioral health to keep the elderly as healthy and active as possible
- Changing ways that society organizes community services to make care more accessible
- Altering a cultural view of aging to make sure all ages are integrated into the fabric of community life

If you are nearing retirement, I urge you to focus on "retirement readiness." While this is a new concept in the retirement community, it comprises more than financial planning. Additionally, it focuses heavily on social, family, emotional, and physical planning for retirement. You cannot simply "retire" anymore; you must begin non-financial retirement planning.

You and your spouse may have focused long and hard on saving and investing to ensure a comfortable retirement. But have you given any thought to what you will do with all that time? Do you have a non-financial plan in place for retirement—which, by the way, could last twenty or thirty years? It is not uncommon for people to be in the home stretch before retirement without a plan for how to spend their days. Sure, they may have talked about trips they want to take, or time they want to spend with family, but a true non-financial retirement plan focuses on you and a new passion for your life that will include meaningful activities to fill your days.

My best advice is this: don't be tempted to focus a great amount of time on your postretirement vacation trip, even if it is a one-month cruise. You and your spouse or partner have many, many years ahead of you that deserve maximum planning now.

My goal with this book is to help you get that Non-Financial Retirement Plan under way. Now. Today.

I will help you create your next lifestyle living plan. I will help you find what truly brings you joy and will add structure to your retirement life. You will create a renewed identity and look forward to each day with excitement.

Let's talk about ten important areas for you to consider as you rewrite your life and form that Non-Financial Retirement Plan.

At the end of each chapter, you will see key notes from that chapter. These are simply a few bullet points that I think are important to remember when you retire.

RETIREMENT PLANNING

Throughout my past eleven years as a financial planner, my clients frequently transition our financial discussions into the non-financial side of retirement. Common topics include downsizing, pets, learning to know a spouse better before retirement, what type of activities or hobbies would be best, and how much involvement to have in the community.

Sometimes, people ask me what I think about constant traveling versus living in a community or what I think of retirement communities. I realize that there is a lot to think about before you retire and taking that first step is a huge move forward for anyone looking at retirement. Recently, I have added non-financial retirement planning as a standard part of preretirement financial planning with all of my clients. I believe our discussions have opened my clients' eyes to things they have never thought about.

Hopefully, this book will become a guide for you as you embark on your own retirement planning; maybe the book will hold a place in your reference library once you do retire.

Let's talk about some of the chapters you will read in this book.

DEFINE YOUR SENSE OF PURPOSE-GET TO KNOW YOU

Retirement is not an event; it is a new life stage and the transition can be challenging if you don't have a plan. Find that "aha" moment when you get to know you. Don't get caught up in the idea that you will just let each day happen. You did not do that in your career and you certainly don't want to do that now.

Just as you controlled your career, you can control your new life stage—retirement. Knowing what you want to do in retirement is a great challenge for most people.

You may have been accustomed to setting goals in your career and probably succeeded in achieving those goals; you were very proud of this. In retirement, you will only account to yourself and not have the same drivers you had in your job. For this reason, you must get to know you and take the first year of retirement to focus on your sense of purpose.

Believe in yourself. Believe in what you really want to do all of the time. Do something! Set goals for you. Don't try to set long-term goals for the next ten years. Begin with short-term goals for one week, then one month, and then six months. You may have decided to do some consulting or mentoring when you retire. Take the first week to determine where you might offer your consulting skills. Build your future on your past if possible. You spent many years becoming skilled in your career. Or if you always wanted to build a small sailboat, take the first week to find the plans and research the materials.

KEEP THAT MENTAL SHARPNESS

Take care of your memory. Our brains do shrink as we age, but new research shows that this process does not have to go hand-in-hand with a decrease in cognitive ability. It is possible to enhance existing brain pathways and even create new ones as one ages.

Develop resilience. Keep a positive mood and a sense of well-being. Wellness is more than being free from illness; it is a dynamic process of evolving and growing. Maintaining wellness in your life is important to ensuring quality of life, especially in retirement. Everything you do and every emotion you feel relate to your well-being, and your well-being affects your actions and emotions. Your physical and mental well-being requires 100 percent of your attention as you age. We will review some of the many ways you can maintain total well-being in retirement.

Staying physically fit through daily exercise is something that also plays into your mental sharpness. You have heard the expression, "If you don't use it, you will lose it." This expression pertains to every part of your body, including your brain. Stay fit physically and mentally.

FIND THAT KID AGAIN

Old is passé. Stop worrying about your chronological age all the time. One of my pet peeves with many retirees is that they constantly stress how old they are and what they can no longer do or will no longer do. It is time to stress what you can do and what you want to do. Go have some fun. Take ballroom dancing lessons or square dancing lessons, or learn to play the guitar as you have always wanted. Find your creative juices again, bring back spontaneity, make new friends and have some fun. Kick up your heels and don't be afraid of what others think. As a matter of fact, dress however you want; there is no such thing as "senior dress." If you like shorts and sandals, go for it. But if you want to dress fancy, dress fancy. Do what makes you feel good. Leave room in your heart to find that kid again.

Get out there! Let me give you a few ideas on how you can stay socially connected and plan playdates for yourself. After reading the chapter, you will probably have a few ideas of your own. A friend of mine built himself a potato gun. "What is a potato gun?" you ask; I did, too. You load the gun with potatoes and shoot them in the air. They then land all over the place and the wildlife that lives in his area seem to enjoy them. Why not just scatter potatoes? Why shoot them? Shooting potatoes is a game that he loves and his grandchildren get a big kick out of him when he gets out the potato gun. He found a way to be a kid again.

ENJOY LEISURE IN MODERATION

Maybe you will get in the habit of rising early and taking a long walk every morning. Maybe you are back to running again. Maybe you always get the first tee time. Whatever it is, you might have a plan to get out there and jumpstart your day.

One argument I often hear from my clients is that they are looking forward to doing nothing and just "hanging out." They don't want to rush anymore like they did in their pre-retirement life. Leisure is good in moderation, but as we all know, too much of anything is never a good thing. Maybe ditch the remote to keep you from turning on the TV too much or lying down on that couch too often. One of the challenges of retirement is how to spend your time. When you begin to make that preretirement plan, think about your physical health and how to keep your mind and body at peak performance. Daily exercise is a great way to begin filling in your calendar and yes, your mind will appreciate the exercise as much as your body. Finding ways to serve others is also a key component of a happy retirement volunteering is discussed later in the book but there are other aspects of service such as service within your own families, churches and communities. I have found that my clients that are the happiest in retirement are actively involved giving back to others in some capacity. Giving back to others helps you feel better about yourself and helps those around you feel better about themselves. Whether it is offering to babysit for your family or your neighbors or helping with a church or community event it will be beneficial for your mind and soul to serve those around you. See the appendix for a couple of websites that will give you opportunities to serve if you are needing help.

FLEXIBILITY IN YOUR BODY AND YOUR MIND
Daily exercise is more than simply staying in shape, it also adds flexibility to your body and flexibility prevents injuries as you age. When I speak with my clients about a nonfinancial plan, I usually put "plan regular exercise" in the

number-one spot. The Centers for Disease Control and Prevention reports that over 250,000 older people are hospitalized for hip fractures; most of these injuries are caused by falls. Falls can cause broken bones, especially wrist, arm, ankle, and hip fractures. When a person is less active, they become weaker and this increases the chances of falling. My moral of these facts is, keep your flexibility by exercising your total body on a regular basis. Exercising your thumb on the remote is not enough. I also suggest to my married clients that finding physical activities that you and your spouse can do together might be a nice idea. Not only will you plan regular exercise for both of you, but also you will develop more time together. This is different from the busy times you both had when you were working or raising a family.

THE BALANCING ACT IN RELATIONSHIPS

Retirement offers a great time to get to know your spouse again, something that may be challenging at first. You may find out that you each have a plan on what you want to do in your retirement. The best way to address each other's plan is to communicate on a regular basis.

Share with each other what you would like to do in your retirement. Your plan to rebuild that old Corvette is probably not something that will interest your wife, or your wife's plan to join a garden club may not be something that would interest you.

I usually speak with my clients about relationships during non-financial retirement planning, as I don't think folks realize that when they begin to spend every day together without a plan, conflicts in the relationship can arise. My number-one suggestion for the relationship-balancing act is to "give each other space." Find times together, but leave room between you.

Whether staying in your own home or relocating to a smaller home, leave room for where you can be you and your wife can be she. These spaces will present a blank canvas to each of you where you can create something new.

The space idea should also apply to your calendar. Leave some blank time for that spontaneity. "Let's go listen to that special jazz band today." Or "How about a trip to the beach to watch the promise of a beautiful sunset?"

Relationship-balancing not only applies to you and your partner, but also to you and your extended family or friends. Communication is truly the conduit to relationship-balance in retirement. Don't assume that your family members know your plan for retirement. Your children may have planned on you being a regular babysitter for your grandchildren. Have that chat before you retire. Set the boundaries early.

Some of my clients actually want to spend their retirement caring for grandchildren full time and that is fine. You may have waited years to have family time finally, and this is your plan for your retirement. That is wonderful and if this works for you and your spouse, move on with your plan.

The importance of communication in any relationship leads me into my final discussion in the book. I spend a lot of time discussing your *legacy*—what you will leave behind. Your legacy is not only financial, but also your story and your wishes for your family and friends after you are gone.

Many of my clients have never even thought about leaving a legacy—most of us probably believe people will remember us in many different ways, and an estate plan will take care of the financial side of things.

There is far more to your legacy that you can control now. You can share your wishes for your extended family if you want, and you can explain in your own words how you feel about your wonderful life lived and what your wishes are for their future. By taking the time to write a Love Letter Legacy, you can share all of your detailed information. The legacy chapter goes into detail about what to think about before you write the letter and how to begin it. I am also providing a sample of a Love Letter Legacy in the Appendix to help you.

Another idea that I think might be a good project is to write your life story. I know many of you might say, "What? I am not a writer." But if you spend a little time every day thinking about some important events in your life, you might be surprised at how much you do have to share. I think your family might be very interested in reading about your past, and you might also find this project enlightening.

So, much of this Introduction is food for thought, and you might very well want to jump in and begin to write. What an amazing gift this would be for your family.

A LAST WORD

I would like to leave you with a few thoughts and questions that you might want to ask yourself before you retire.

- **Remember that retirement is not an event; it is a new life chapter for you**. Hopefully, it will last for another twenty to thirty years, maybe as long as your career did. Maybe consider retirement your new career and the canvas before you is blank. Pick up that paint brush and see where it leads you as you begin to plan your days. You may only paint the next month on that canvas, but that is OK.

- **Be patient with yourself and with your spouse or partner**. Wading into unknown waters sometimes requires small steps; take those small steps carefully. Communicate often, and become an excellent listener. Learn to compromise.

- **Take time to get to know you**. Who is the real you? You no longer have others to please every day whether you agree with them or not. You only answer to yourself now. What do you want to be your purpose in life? What is your passion in life? Find that reason to get up every day and get on with painting your canvas.

CHAPTER 1

RETIREMENT

*"Get excited and enthusiastic about your own
dream. This excitement is like a forest fire—you
can smell it, taste it, and see if from a mile away."*

—DENIS WAITLEY, MOTIVATIONAL SPEAKER

YOU'VE DECIDED TO RETIRE

YOU HAVE MADE that life-changing decision; you will retire.
Whether you chose full retirement or phased retirement,
you have definitely made the retirement decision. For the
past many years, your focus—aside from your job—has been
to save, save, save and build a sufficient nest egg that will provide for your life in retirement. You have done an amazing
job with sound financial planning for your future. You are
set financially, but do you have a plan for how you will spend
your time in your retirement? Have you given much thought
to the non-financial side of retirement, or will you let your
days fall simply into place?

You may be looking at twenty to thirty years in retirement. How will you stay engaged and excited about your future years? Believe it or not, there is far more to ensuring an enjoyable retirement than just having enough money. You will not have your career identity anymore in the same way that you did before retirement. While you may have chosen phase retirement in an effort to hold on to your career, you will still be retired, and your calendar will not be filled with as many nine-to-five career responsibilities in the way it was before.

There are a few things you may want to think about as you plan your retirement. Consider these non-financial factors that could impact your quality of life:

- Do you have a plan to find meaning in your life (life's purpose) after retirement?
- What about your relationships? How will retirement affect your marriage, your family time, and your life-long friendships?
- Have you given any thought to how your transition to retirement will affect you emotionally? Retirement is a huge adjustment for people who are accustomed to working over forty hours a week and have created a sense of identity through their professions.

If you are preparing for phased retirement, you may be able to explore possible interests outside of work while continuing your profession, even though part time.

A dentist friend of mine has been able to do very well with phased retirement. His partner, now the senior partner, runs the practice and he works only in the summertime, which allows the senior partner to take long vacations. He has purchased a condo in Florida and spends five months at his southern condo playing golf every day. This was his plan and it works very well for him.

Another acquaintance of mine retired from being an electrician at the age of fifty-five, but because his wife was still working, he decided to get a commercial driver's license, and now he drives a school bus every day. It is far less stressful than his career as an electrician, and he now has summers off and is home every day by three. Driving a school bus makes him feel young again, as he really enjoys the kids. The extra cash helps as well.

Unfortunately, not everyone has figured out how to add to his or her lives in retirement. Another couple I know— both schoolteachers—retired together last year. They had no plan other than financial, and now they trip over each other all day long. As the wife put it, "Every day is so long." This couple reports total boredom in retirement. Facing too many empty hours can be an emotional shock and definitely throw you off balance.

Another client of mine is single and financially very sound and can retire at any time. However, she does not know what to do when she retires, so she continues to work with a different outlook. She is on the "2-10-12 plan." If you make her angry 2 times by 10 a.m., she will retire at 12 p.m. With this mind-set, she lets a lot more roll off her back, she continues to work, and maintains those friendships. She has a purpose to get up for each day.

Make no bones about it, retirement is a major life step forward—a transition into your next life stage. Careful planning for the non-financial and emotional sides of your life can help ease this transition and prepare you for an amazing and fulfilling retirement lifestyle. One suggestion is this: Even though you will be retired, don't walk away from your past—build upon it. (See the Appendix for helpful resources)

BUILD YOUR FUTURE ON YOUR PAST

Find that "aha" moment to help you plan a fulfilling and meaningful retirement.

Human beings experience life stages: infancy to childhood to adolescence to young adulthood to primary career years and then to "elder hood." Once you reach "elder hood," you have spent the past sixty-five to seventy years collecting valuable information, life experiences, wisdom, education, and common sense. You have met people along the way who have impacted your life in some way. You may have a family whose lives you have guided and maybe continue to guide. You may have risen to the top of your field with total dedication to your career. Finally, you may have nurtured strong, lifelong friendships and relationships that have supported and guided you through the past many years and have been the foundation of your social life.

Your first realization is, "Wow, what an amazing past I have," along with the massive amount of smarts you now possess, in many ways. Consider what a waste it would be if you did nothing with that amazing accumulation of life experiences.

A client of mine retired recently from a nuclear power plant where he worked at a job he loved. To stay busy after retirement and to stay in the game, he returns to the power plant twice a year to work for one month at a time. This allows him to stay connected with his previous coworkers socially, and he knows this helps to keep him mentally sharp. He and his wife don't really need the money, but it is nice to have the extra cash to help them increase their travel funds.

Human beings are living longer now and taking better care of themselves in many ways. Their bodies are not as worn out as they were once. You may even want to extend your primary career years into your seventies or eighties— maybe not in your career job as it was in the past, but in other ways by thinking about what you have, what you enjoy, what you want to learn, and how you want to live as you transition to the retirement stage of your life.

You may have heard from others that they are so busy in retirement they don't know how they ever had time to build a career. They may have planned how to fill their days with meaningful focus, or they may simply be gliding from one day to another and letting life happen. In reality, doing various projects around the house, puttering in hobbies, and enjoying leisure time gets old pretty quickly. After the honeymoon period is over, what do you plan to do? Don't just hope for the best, spend time now—before retirement—and consider the possibilities, opportunities, and challenges.

Maybe for the first time, give some serious thought to finding your purpose in life. Here is an example to illustrate this even further. A gentleman retired several years ago at the age of sixty-two. He and his wife have two grown children and three grandchildren. When recently asked what he was doing with himself in retirement, he mentioned that he and his wife spent a lot of time "catching up with things on the Internet and watching a lot of TV." Over time, their physical health began to deteriorate and as a result when they are not surfing the web, they are spending time at doctors' appointments. Maybe they have been researching illnesses, getting those illnesses, and then spending time at doctors to treat the illnesses. Generally speaking, retirees probably do see their doctors more, and retirees probably do research on the Internet more. But this couple seems to have no direction in retirement and therefore, their retirement lacks a passion. In addition to the way they spend their days, they report that they spend very little time with their children or grandchildren and in fact spend very little time doing anything of substance at all.

Don't find yourself with empty days in retirement. Get to know you. Find your passion and go for it. Here are a few questions to get you thinking about planning your future in retirement:

1. **What were you passionate about in your youth but didn't have time then to add to your busy life?** Was it dancing, writing, woodworking, or maybe something else?

2. **What would you choose to do if you had no other commitments on your time?** Teaching night school? Farming? Working with animals? Caretaking? Creating that woodworking shop?

3. **Do you have strong interests in any of these activities?** Writing? Singing? Dancing? Painting? Mentoring? Volunteering? Continuing education? Higher learning?

4. **Is there another specific area of interest that you would like to pursue?** Believe it or not, you now have the time to do something you have always wanted.

5. **Do you want to spend more regular time with your grandchildren?** Maybe you have wanted to be a bigger part of their lives but never had the opportunity to make that commitment.

6. **Here are harder questions.** Where do you see yourself at age seventy-five? Age eighty? Age eighty-five?

7. **Do you and your spouse share interests?** If so, do you have a plan to pursue those interests? If you do not share interests, how will you manage your own individual interests and still spend time together?

8. **Are you willing to put yourself in situations and circumstances that expose you to new and different opportunities?** Maybe more dedication to physical

exercise will require more time and effort, or learning a skill from the bottom up—such as gardening or woodworking; or maybe you want to take up tennis or golf—something you have never done but always wanted to try.

9. **Have you thought much about how you want to spend your final days?** This is not a question many want to answer, but if you become more spiritual in your retirement, you may think about this phase of your life.

Finding your purpose in life in retirement may not be so easy, and it may take time to discover, but you will know it when you can say your purpose in life is timeless (you could do this forever), tireless (you never get tired of doing this), and causes infectious energy (you can't wait to get started every day). This is your "aha" moment.

Retirement is an opportunity to hit the reset button—get out there and do it. You finally have time. Someone once said, "When things fall apart, the pieces sometimes land in a better shape than they ever were." Retirement can be like this if you work to find that special purpose.

GET TO KNOW *YOU*

Human beings do not thrive doing nothing all day long. Remember someone once saying, "If you don't use it, you lose it"? This not only applies to specific muscles but to you as a whole. You are capable of so much more than simply leisure and that is what you need to find—that sense of purpose in your life. Begin by getting to know yourself on a very intimate level. Your sense of purpose must interlock with what you think is important in your life. Only this objective will nourish you.

Many people have never had more than a fleeting chance to take a serious, close look at what they value, truly.

Over the years, business responsibilities and missions have left little time for you to focus on what you value most in life. Knowing yourself—knowing who you are and what you value personally and knowing what makes your heart sing are big parts of getting retirement right. Knowing and understanding who you are may not be easy and it will take some effort on your part.

You have probably spent most of your adult life striving to please many others—bosses, spouses, parents, kids, friends, neighbors, and so on. Acknowledging to yourself what really lights your fire was most likely not part of that drill. After retirement, the need to please others shifts. Instead of being vital to a company all of the time, you can now choose where you want to focus your identity. Now, you may want to become more vital in your community and or your church. This is your time to create your new identity.

You may find that expensive relocations often don't work out; exotic travel may leave you wondering, "What's the point?", and purchases can leave you feeling empty. To have a satisfying retirement, you have to be who you really are and be comfortable in your own skin.

DISCOVER YOUR PURPOSE, MAKE A PLAN, AND LIVE YOUR RETIREMENT WITH PASSION

You may say to this idea of finding your life purpose, "I have a purpose in life. I want to spend leisure time now, something I could never do." Leisure is not an active sport; it may quickly produce boredom and maybe even depression. You will be surprised when you notice that finding your purpose is a feeling that continues to pull at you. Sometimes, it might be right in front of your eyes, but you never allowed yourself to see it. For example, a school nurse found herself doing more and more work with foster children. When she retired, she realized that she felt most in sync with hands-on work helping foster children and families. That was the part she enjoyed about her work—not the school-day administration per se but the time helping foster children find a place and nurturing them as they grew into adulthood. Helping people was her true calling, and it was staring her right in the face the whole time.

You may be thinking, "I am very happy, I don't need anything more." It's important not to confuse seeking happiness with finding your purpose. The highs and lows of happiness will ebb and flow in your life, but finding your life purpose is more profound—it is an underlying sense of overall satisfaction or what some might term "pure joy."

Happiness is temporary; joy is not. When you know who you are on the inside and understand your true values, secret desires, and imagination, you will achieve your true-life purpose.

There are a few conditions in life when a sense of purpose may fade: unemployment, professional stagnation, financial straits, romantic straits, after the death of a loved one, and in retirement. A client of mine became a victim of fading life purpose after retirement. Then one day, he was tapped by a local education organization to help a kindergarten with literacy coaching that would help students with test scores and morale. He not only helped the students, but also brightened his own life. He became significantly healthier both mentally and physically. His depression all but disappeared. He became more physically mobile, had more stamina all day long, and his flexibility increased. He also reported better cognitive functioning and improvement in his memory.

Another client was pushed into an early retirement. Financially, he and his wife were comfortable. However, they found their retirement very dull and boring, and as a result, retirement was taxing on their marriage. One day, they decided to build a cabin, not buy an existing cabin, but actually build the cabin themselves. They had no background in any type of building, so they decided to buy a kit for building a cabin and together, they learned something new. This new activity and joint learning project reignited their marriage and gave them a new purpose for many years. It took a long time to build the cabin, and now they enjoy it immensely with family.

Many financial advisers offer help with a "Financial Retirement Plan," but what is not in their skill sets is how to help you develop your "Non-Financial Retirement Plan." This type of plan is something that you and your spouse (or you, alone) must develop. (See the Appendix for a template on how to develop your Non-Financial Retirement Plan.)

A lengthy plan to immerse yourself in volunteer work may already be on your calendar, but volunteering only works when you are doing something you in which you believe. Just to volunteer for volunteering's sake may soon become old, and you may find it difficult to continue. If you love volunteering, focus on volunteering in an area of interest where you passion lies. By following your passion to give back, you will be rewarded with far more than money. When you intentionally devote your time, energy and resources to worthy causes, you will be more fully able to live a more passionate, purposeful life- rich in wellness that comes from helping others and giving back to causes that you care deeply about.

It has been said, "If you laugh a lot, when you get older, your wrinkles will be in the right places." There is still time to change where those wrinkles are if currently, they are not in the right places.

KEY NOTES FOR CHAPTER ONE

- Don't walk away from your past; build on it.
- Find your life purpose in retirement. Find that "aha" moment.
- Get to know and understand yourself to find your passion.
- Make a Non-Financial Retirement Plan

CHAPTER 2

STAY SHARP MENTALLY AND STRONG PHYSICALLY

"How old would you be if you didn't know how old you were?"

—SATCHEL PAIGE, BASEBALL PLAYER

WELLNESS IS MORE than being free from illness; it is a dynamic process of evolving and growing. Maintaining wellness in your life is very important to ensure quality of life, especially in retirement. Everything you do and every emotion you feel relates to your well-being and your well-being affects your actions and emotions. Optimal wellness calms stress, reduces the risk of illness, and ensures positive interactions. Wellness is more than physical well-being; it is also emotional, social, spiritual, and intellectual well-being. Each dimension of well-being is vital to helping you achieve optimum health.

WELLNESS MATTERS

Physical well-being is probably your number-one goal. You are correct if it takes the number-one position on your list as it is critical for overall well-being and is the most visible of the well-being. You know the old saying, "If you don't have your health, you don't have anything." This is all the more reason to maintain your body and see your health-care provider when necessary. Achieving physical well-being is more than an annual physical; it requires you to do your part. Remember, prevention is key to a healthy retirement. Embrace preventive health care and include things like mammograms, prostate exams, colonoscopies, and flu shots in your life.

- **Get physical**. Dedicate a time every day for physical activity including flexibility practice and endurance. Physical activity can be a mix of leisurely exercise (hiking, biking, walking) and structured exercise (strength training, running, sports).
  My father has a very established and well balanced way of maintaining his physical well-being. Four to five days a week, he rides his bike four miles then hikes five miles and rides his bike four miles home. He does this fairly early each day and is usually home by noon. When he leaves to go hiking, my mom leaves to go walking at the mall before it opens. Not only is each person taking part in some physical exercise, but these activities also allow them a healthy amount of time apart from each other daily while helping both of them maintain good physical health. When they return from their exercises, they eat lunch together, which is their largest meal of the day. Research

continually shows that eating your largest meal for lunch instead of dinner is far healthier for your body. The earlier time in the day allows your body more time to digest your meal and burn the calories before bedtime. Most everyone tends to eat their big meal as evening dinner because of the time constraints of an eight-hour workday. Originally, this habit came about during the Industrial Revolution. Before the Industrial Revolution most people ate lunch as their big meal. Generally speaking, obesity was less of a problem then than it is today. In retirement, you no longer have to live by the big-meal-at-dinner rule.

- **Eat well**. Practice good nutrition and diet on a daily basis that includes nutrient intake (carbohydrates, proteins, fats, vitamins, minerals), fluid intake (water), and foods that promote healthy digestion (fiber-rich foods). Don't restrict any nutrients without a health-care professional's recommendation.

- **Enjoy in moderation**. Reduce your consumption of alcohol, especially if it appears to alter your mood or bodily processes. Many fad diets exist that come and go. Most of these diets involve eliminating certain things from your menu. Realistically, moderation in all things is good, and if you don't practice this now, it is a good time to begin. If you like to have a chocolate chip cookie occasionally for dessert, have one—just don't have a dozen cookies. You can find research that shows how red meat can be bad for your digestion;

however, you can also find studies that report red meat in proper proportions is good for you. Again, it's a pretty good rule to live a life of moderation.

- **Pay attention to medical needs**. Address minor medical ailments or injuries and seek emergency care when needed.
- **Get that R&R**. Get plenty for relaxation and high-quality sleep. National Sleep Foundation in an article titled "National Sleep Foundation Recommends New Sleep Times"[2] recommends that sleep last from seven to nine hours per night for adults age 65 and older. Consistent sleep that is much shorter or longer than this duration or is low quality may need to be addressed by a health professional. Not getting enough sleep can have a much greater negative impact on your life than simply causing you to be tired throughout the day. According to a report published on WebMD, "Ten Things to Hate About Sleep Loss,"[3] lack of sleep can cause auto accidents; lack of sex drive; and serious health problems such as heart disease, heart failure, stroke, or diabetes. Lack of sleep can also cause depression, cause aging of your skin, and make you forgetful. The good news is that in retirement, you are in charge of your own schedule, and you can now make getting enough sleep a priority.

Emotional well-being conveys your ability to cope effectively with stress and understand your feelings. You can achieve this by paying attention to your personal needs—your own self-care. Know when you need to relax and answer this call. Reduce stress in your life. You are retired now; you don't have to jump up for the needs of everyone else anymore. You must work on developing your own inner resources that will help you control unneeded stress and take care of you.

Life has a way of throwing more and more things at people who don't push back. You may have been this way throughout your professional career or even with your family's demands. Work to control this now and pay attention to the calls of your body when it says, "I am stressed, I need to relax." Do it. Relax. Go for a walk. Breathe.

Try meditation, it is a wonderful way of quieting the chatter in your brain. Learning to meditate will take a little time, but it is worth it and once you learn to meditate, you will rely on that special time just for you every day. Meditation is part of *mindfulness*, which means to be here now—don't be anywhere else.

Practice meditation as part of your daily time just for you. Remember to treat your emotional injuries when they occur. Some people pray often and believe that prayer is a substitute for meditation. This belief is actually not true; make sure to incorporate meditation before and after prayer. This practice will make both praying and meditating more meaningful. (See the Appendix for additional resources.)

When your emotional well-being is not doing well, you may find that you are more vulnerable to things like failure, rejection, anxiety, and stress. Try not to self-criticize, and protect your self-esteem when it is low by practicing self-compassion. Allow your self-esteem to recover and your entire mental health will get a boost. Focus on things that are in your control to balance out any defeatist thoughts, and you will avoid feelings of failure. Do what is necessary to improve your chances of success.

Brooding thoughts can get the best of almost anyone if allowed to steep. Stewing over upsetting events can only make you feel worse than you probably do already. As soon as you begin to focus on a negative thought, distract yourself immediately. Take a walk or go for a run and wait for your mood to recover.

Reflect on this quote: *"The way to happiness: keep your heart free from hate, your mind free from worry, live simply, expect little, give much."* Irishman, Barney O'Lavin, who founded the Flint Group.

Social well-being will help you create a support network by performing social roles effectively and comfortably. You will be able to develop encouraging relationships with peers who may be new in your life. If you relocate after retirement, social well-being will be very important in helping you to establish new forms of socializing and new friendships.

Try not to limit your social life to your lifetime partner and a circle of close friends. Get out there—meet new people and get involved in social events. There are always conferences, exhibitions, and movie premiers taking place somewhere. Remain dynamic and socially active. Avoid social isolation.

Social media such as Facebook can be a healthy way of reconnecting with family and old friends. Use it wisely and avoid getting overly opinionated with your posts, as this might offend some people who might otherwise be good friends. Remember that no one agrees with opinions of others 100 percent of the time. A client of mine reported that she was able to reconnect with extended family members after fifty years. She used to spend time with them when she was a child but had lost all contact. She and her family now share old family photos. This same woman was also able to reconnect with some of her close friends from high school resulting in the group meeting every six months for lunch and a mini high- school reunion.

Spiritual well-being is something that you may seek in your own way. Being spiritually well means knowing what resources you can use to cope with issues that come up in everyday life. Spiritual wellness allows you to develop a set of values that help you seek meaning and purpose in human existence. Formation of your own faith and hope are part of spiritual well-being, which is a very important part of total well-being.

If you do not adhere to a specific religion, now is a great time to visit various congregations to find one you like. Talk with your friends about their respective churches. If you are seeking a new church, let your friends know up front that you are visiting numerous churches so that you do not offend anyone when you don't pick their church.

There is more to spiritual well-being than just attending church once a week. Make a weekly goal to incorporate at least one thing you learn at church that week into your daily life. If your church isn't giving you ideas, perhaps you might want to visit others.

Intellectual well-being can also be called lifelong learning and is a dimension that you probably do not think too much about...but maybe you should now that you are retired. There are so many opportunities for continued learning through local colleges and universities. Lifelong learning can incorporate non-credit academic classes, travel for education, and higher-education learning. Lifelong learning stimulates your brain and can help to build strong social relationships. Even if you attended college years ago, continued education should remain ongoing forever.

Many libraries offer discussions and classes on various topics. Computer classes are very much in order for retirees. How many times have you avoided computer technology because it was becoming more and more complicated? You might be surprised at how quickly you will catch on when you take a computer class at any level. Most adult schools and many other organizations offer these classes. Some computer stores also offer computer classes. Making the most of your senior years with lifelong learning can help you to do the following:

- Develop your natural abilities
- Live with an open mind
- Crave ongoing learning
- Increase your outward wisdom

- Adapt to change
- Find greater meaning in your life
- Stay involved as an active contributor to society
- Make new friends and establish valuable relationships
- Enrich your life and self-fulfillment

The demands of your career life may have interfered with your desire to get serious about your wellness, but now you have no excuse. Put regular wellness practices on your daily calendar in ink not in pencil.

Most people—no matter what age—want to live a fit and healthy lifestyle, and stay mentally sharp at the top of their game. These goals are especially true for retirees who see all the advertisements of healthy, tanned seniors walking or running along a beach of sparkling white sand and aquamarine waters. The retirees in the photographs appear to be in perfect physical shape, very relaxed, and glowing with enjoyment. Thinking that retirement will ensure this lifestyle for you may be a bit of a challenge unless your life pretty much follows this route already. Maybe think more about how you can become more physically active now that you don't have the daily commitment of a job. Maybe start boosting your vitality.

MAINTAIN YOUR COGNITIVE VITALITY

Cognitive vitality—mental sharpness—is essential to quality of life and survival in your elder years. During normal aging, cognitive changes such as slowed speed of processing information are common; however, there is significant individual inconsistency, and cognitive decline is *not* destined for everyone. Various lifestyle factors and medical *comorbidities* (simultaneous presence of two conditions: aging and another condition) play a major role in and are associated with an individual's tendency toward cognitive decline. Comorbidities that are manageable include diabetes, hypertension, and hyperlipidemia (high concentration of fat in the blood)—all three can contribute to cognitive decline. Other comorbidities such as smoking and excess alcohol intake may also contribute to cognitive decline; avoiding smoking and excess alcohol intake may promote cognitive vitality.

Many positive lifestyle factors that you can control include: lifelong learning, mental and physical exercise, continuing social engagement, stress reduction, and proper nutrition. They are all important factors in promoting cognitive vitality during aging.

More than likely, you can impact your potential to maintain cognitive vitality by making a few lifestyle changes.

1. **Do not smoke,** and if you do smoke, stop. Your health-care provider can help you to stop if you are unable to do this alone. The important thing is to take that first step to stop smoking.

2. **Practice moderation** with alcohol. Health experts say drink no more than one glass of wine a day or abstain completely. That glass of wine at the end of the day with friends or your partner seems like a nice way to

relax. After that, switch to something refreshing like Mojito water (iced water with lime and mint). It is a definite "perk-up."

3. **Get serious about your diabetes, a very serious disorder.** Maintenance and preventive therapy are the keys to managing this debilitating disorder. Get on a serious exercise program, lose weight, and maintain a diabetic diet without fail. Follow the advice of your doctor and monitor your blood sugar often. Meet with the diabetes educator in your physician's office, and ask any questions you have to help you manage your diabetes.

4. **Hypertension is another serious disorder.** It can have life-threatening results if not controlled. Take your medication as directed by your health-care provider, get lots of exercise, and start using a salt alternative.

DAILY CHOICES MATTER

Have you noticed a very common theme throughout the lifestyle issues being mentioned here? Daily physical exercise and good nutrition are the common themes throughout this book. As you age, you must get serious about your physical and mental health exercise and nutrition based habits don't just happen on their own. You are the only person who has control over management of these attributes.

There are many things that you are can control, especially your physical and mental health, which contribute to longevity. Guidance offered in the first two chapters of this book includes things that you can implement by making daily choices to do or not to do something. Take things in small pieces, set small goals and try to progress every day. If you are overweight, live a very sedentary life and have poor dietary habits when you embark on retirement, chances may be slim that you are will change your lifestyle completely overnight. Small steps are important. Beginning to take those steps is essential if you are going to enjoy a healthy, happy retirement.

Increase your energy by maintaining a healthy body. If food preparation is not your thing and you like to buy pre-pared foods, maybe change your slant on this thinking. If you are able to have a service bring in a healthy meal a day to your home, this may be a benefit to helping you jump-start your healthy eating. (Refer to the Appendix for more resources).

Maybe relook at your day, beginning with breakfast. *Wake up to a better breakfast.* You have probably heard over and over again that breakfast is the most important meal of the day; it might even boost your energy, help your memory levels, and impact how long you live. Instead of grabbing a cup of coffee and a donut or that plain bowl of cereal, why not put some colorful fruit together. A blue-berry-rich diet may help improve your motor skills and fight diseases. Actually, a berry-rich diet is often referred to as a *superfood diet.* How about adding a bowl of oatmeal to the powerful fruit? Not only does this look inviting, but oatmeal also has been touted for years as a cholesterol reduction product. This beautiful meal is now adding up to include two of the healthiest nutrition items—fruit and grains.

Don't forget about eggs, which contain essential B vitamins, biotin, choline, and proteins. For years, reports cautioned that eggs should be avoided because of their high cholesterol. Newer studies show that healthy men and women who consume an egg a day actually do not experience any negative health issues. You be the judge here, but certainly given the positive nutrients associated with eggs, it might be a good idea to include them in you breakfast regimen a couple of times a week. Add some whole-grain toast and maybe a piece of fruit, and again you have a sumptuous, healthy, eye-appealing breakfast.

Variety is the spice of life! Lunch and dinner can be just as appealing, healthful, and easy as breakfast. Try to include grains, green vegetables, nuts, fruits, fish, and olive oil in your meals. There are books and books about nutritious meals and many of them now stress the Mediterranean diet, which includes all of the above. Remember that moderation is the key here and don't think you have to give up red meat and ice cream—just don't have them every day!

Consider changing your larger meal to lunch instead of dinner at least on the days where that is convenient for you. The science and logic to eating your large meal earlier in the day does make sense. Many other countries, where obesity is less of a problem, already follow this practice.

Hydrate, hydrate, hydrate and more hydration. As you age, your body changes, and you actually need more water in your diet—not less. Drink lots of water every day. Find a refillable water bottle or jug that you like, and take it with you everywhere. You will soon see that you will drink more water. (See the Appendix for more resources.)

STAY SHARP MENTALLY FOREVER

Exercise your brain just like you exercise your body. Keep your mind sharp and your memory intact. Mental exercise such as learning new things or pursuing activities that are stimulating intellectually may strengthen your brain-cell networks and help preserve mental functions.

A client of mine takes daily hikes and brings scripture passages with him. While on the trail, he memorizes the verses. This not only helps him in spiritual well-being, but it also keeps his mind sharp. There are many studies that suggest keeping your brain active and exercising it by memorization or simply challenging it in any way can help reduce the chances of Alzheimer's disease later in life. Much of the ongoing research in this area consistently reports that keeping your brain active will make you smarter now even if it doesn't reduce the chance of getting Alzheimer's disease or dementia later in life.

Another idea is to listen to TED talks (a non-profit devoted to ideas worth spreading) or podcasts while exercising instead of listening to music or watching TV. TED talks are three- to ten-minute talks from the newest and most interesting experts on topics that range from global warming, to the future of robots, to how to make the world a better place. Basically, TED talks have something of interest for everyone, and new talks are posted every day. In today's world, accessing TED talks is very easily accomplished with a smartphone or other electronic device. Schedule a class at the Apple Store and learn how to access TED talks, or chances are, friends or family members know how to do this already.

Continue education. Self-efficacy is associated with mental sharpness among older persons because continued learning creates a neural reserve of denser, stronger nerve-cell connections that increase the brain's ability to compensate for age-related changes in neural structure and function. Better-educated people also may tend to lead brain-healthier lifestyles.

Keep busy and engaged. Work toward a lifelong habit of learning and engaging in mentally challenging activities. Intellectual enrichment and learning stimulate the brain to make more connections. The more connections, the more resilient the brain stays. Some types of mentally challenging activities include learning a new language or a new craft.

Stay connected. People who are socially engaged are also likely to be more active mentally and physically—both of which are beneficial for your brain. Establish and maintain close ties with others to maintain mental skills and memory. Social engagement such as social interactions and mentally engaging activities go hand in hand. Volunteering or tutoring school kids may be just the activity for you. Social relationships are important in times of stress and can provide you with support when needed. Social support can come from family, friends, caregivers, or the religious community. (See the Appendix for resources.)

TAKE CARE OF YOUR MEMORY

The following are a few simple strategies that might help you improve your ability to remember things when needed:

- *Write it down.* This repeats the information that you want to remember, and it also offers a visual reminder.
- *Focus.* Concentrate on what you are doing. Ignore distractions and interruptions. Pay attention to what you are trying to learn or remember.
- *Repeat.* Repetition strengthens the connections in your brain.
- *Visualize.* Reinforce brain connections by visualizing what you are trying to remember.
- *Organize.* Always keep things in the same place and return them to that place when you use them. Put your keys on a hook by the door and your wallet in a basket on your dresser to help you stay organized.
- *Prioritize.* Multitasking may become more difficult as you age, so carefully planning your time and prioritizing your activities will become more important. Preplanning can help reduce stress.

KEY NOTES FOR CHAPTER TWO

- Embrace preventive health care. Maintaining your health is everything.
- Understand the importance of all the dimensions of wellness.
- Impact your potential to maintain cognitive vitality through lifestyle changes.
- Know simple strategies to protect your memory as you age.

CHAPTER 3

FIND THAT KID AGAIN

"Retire from work, but not from life."

—Dr. M. K. Soni, Executive Director &
Dean, Faculty of Engineering and Technology

When was the last time you really let loose and played like a child? Start waking with that childlike enthusiasm again, and do away with the unnecessary tension, anxiousness, and stress. You are now retired!

PLAN THOSE PLAYDATES (FOR YOU)

Make new friends. Socializing will energize and nourish you. Find ways to plan playdates for you with others. Fill up your calendar.

By now, you know that physical exercise is the number-one ticket to ensuring a long, happy life. Try getting involved with a group at your local YMCA or a sport club in your town such as golf or bocce. Or find a walking group that you can join every day. If you live near a mall, usually, there is a morning group that walks through the mall before the stores open. Maybe even start your own social club that exercises outdoors on a regular basis. Maybe you even follow up the exercise with a coffee or lunch date, or maybe you have your fellow exercisers back to your home for lunch!

Maybe you like to cook for others and if you do, this now opens lots of times for playdates. There are endless opportunities for filling your calendar with playdates that involve sports and exercise.

If exercise is not really your thing, maybe you prefer immersing yourself in the arts. Art appreciation clubs abound around the world (www.art-appreciation.meetup.com). You are sure to meet some folks with interests like yours through this opportunity. If a meet-up club does not exist in your area, why not think about starting one?

A business acquaintance of mine always loved to cook for everyone. His specialty was great Italian meals. Whenever we had long evening business meetings, he would bring something wonderful like lasagna or sausage and peppers. When he retired, he was at a complete loss as to how to make new friends. As it turned out, he and his wife moved closer to their grandkids after retirement but knew no one in their new community. His wife suggested to him that he prepare an Italian meal and invite a few neighbors over. His eyes lit up and he was on his way. From that one Sunday afternoon meal, he offered to do more, and when he began volunteering as a driver for a senior center, he met people who were more than happy to enjoy his Italian meals that he now prepared at the Senior Center several times a month. His wife became involved in helping him with preparation and serving the meals. They now had very full social calendars, and they were enjoying every minute of every day, doing what they loved.

Cooking for others is a wonderful, creative outlet and a perfect way to get those playdates going. Maybe you have always wanted to learn more about cooking. Today, cooking schools are numerous, and you will probably find one in your area. The classes offer a perfect opportunity to meet others with the same interests as your own. Perhaps you want to learn more about how to use a smoker or to learn new grilling techniques but never had the time. Now you have the time. Maybe you will become known as the grill/smoker expert in the neighborhood!

We all need to do what we enjoy rather than what is a chore. Sharing our enjoyment with others can be a vital connection in retirement to developing new friends and filling up the social calendar.

Someone once said that enthusiasm is catching. Others will want to be a part of your enthusiasm for life when you get out there.

STAY CONNECTED SOCIALLY

Build relationships and social networks. Multiple recent studies reveal an ever- strengthening link between social interaction and mental and physical well-being for seniors.

Socialization is important for any age, beginning with infancy; however, maintaining socialization is most challenging for seniors when opportunities seem to decrease, especially if you find you must rely on others for transportation. You may have spent a great amount of time in the company of others in the workplace or raising children. An active social lifestyle is more important than ever in helping to maintain a sharp mind, remaining connected to the world around you, increasing feelings of happiness, and developing a sense of belonging.

"Social contact may be as effective as physical activity in improving mood and quality of life."

—UNKNOWN

A study published in the *Annals of Family Medicine*, reported that "Social contact may be as effective as physical activity in improving mood and quality of life," and "social participation and social support networks are paramount to long-term positive outcomes and psychological well-being for older people."[4] Another study conducted by Marid-Jeanne Kergoat—a professor at the Université de Montréal—and her peers discovered a correlation between food intake and social interaction. The study revealed, "...patients ate more when social interactions were friendly and lively..." [5]An active social life can boost the immune system, lower blood pressure, and reduce physical pain that is reinforced by depression.

Another recent article published by AARP reported that seniors in large groups are more likely to encourage healthy habits among each other, including exercise. Sufficient social interaction is far more than periodic interaction with family members or caregivers; it is participation or consistent engagement with others, primarily your peers.

Here are a few ideas that may help you stay connected socially:

1. **Learn to use the Internet**. If you do not use a computer already to communicate with others on social networks or research activities in your area, maybe get a computer and learn to use the Internet now. Some people shy away from computer use and feel they are OK without the computer; however, in today's world, this is the way to stay current with what is happening and communicate with others through social networks such as Facebook. You may be surprised to find that many of your acquaintances are there already. The Internet is also a way to find social groups that offer ways for you to meet new people with the same interests as your own. The Internet is a way of life today. Any local computer store offers classes, especially the Apple Store where Apple School has many opportunities for learning. Adult schools and libraries also offer computer learning. There is no excuse now—learn to use the Internet and get connected socially.

2. **Join clubs and groups**. There are so many opportunities through your local YMCA, community center, senior center, library, and sport clubs to join a
   group. You have only to investigate what each offers
   and then become involved. If shooting and guns are
   your thing, you can usually find a club or group at
   the local indoor or outdoor shooting range. You are
   likely to find others with similar interests and mind-
   sets to yours and can expand your social network
   through your hobbies. Or you may want to join a
   book club, or learn a new sport such as pickle ball.
   These courts are popping up everywhere throughout
   the United States and provide great exercise as well
   as social interaction. Again, the opportunities are
   endless.

3. **Volunteer**. There is no limit to social interaction when
   you volunteer. You can decide the type of volunteering you have always thought about, and contact that
   facility or organization in your area. Undoubtedly,
   you will meet many other volunteers who have the
   same interests as your own.

4. **Get a pet**. You may have always wanted a dog and
   never had the time to train the pet or spend time
   exercising him or her. Now you have the time and
   you can get involved with others who have pets by
   walking or even training events. You may even want
   to go so far as raising or showing a specific breed.
   Dog shows abound and if this is your interest, you can
   get as involved as you want.

5. **Learn a new skill**. Classes of any type can stimulate your mind as well as offer opportunities for interaction with fellow students and teachers. Usually, continuing education classes are available at your local college.

6. **Join a church**. Churches will be a main source of socialization opportunities throughout your life—especially in retirement. Many churches offer senior-group and single-group activities such as potluck dinners, socials, and field trips. Through a church, you can join bible study groups as well as become involved in humanitarian causes and local service opportunities. There are many people that use the church as their spiritual foundation as well as a large part of their social connections. As discussed previously, reach out to your neighbors, friends, and family about their churches, and this will help you narrow down your search. I have numerous clients who plan to go on service and proselyting missions for the LDS church once they retire. This is rewarding in multiple ways, it allows them to give back and also meet a lot of new people.

7. **Attend sports events**. Buy tickets, check out the websites, discuss the sport with your friends, and maybe attend the games or events together. Join a bowling team if this has always been something you wanted to do, or find a golf team at your local golf club. Most of the public golf courses offer senior teams or other opportunities.

8. **Stay involved with the outside world**. Get out of your house and be with other people. If you desire healthy

aging, remain engaged—remain in charge of your own life, and participate in the larger community. Be with others and create your own fun.

9. **Become a mentor**. At this stage in your life, you likely have talents that could benefit others. My children enjoy golf lessons from a retired golf pro that comes to their school once a week and teaches golf to elementary aged children. If you know how to run a small business, seek out one in your neighborhood, and offer your services or ideas.

A local financial advising firm meets once a quarter with a retired financial adviser just to bounce ideas off of him and over time, the firm and its advisors have developed a great friendship with him. This scenario is very rewarding for both the firm and the retired financial adviser. Sometimes, mentorships start out as a free service and eventually transition into a paid consulting arrangement. If this opportunity sounds interesting to you, and you want to market your services, it might be a good idea to give it a go. Several of my clients were nurses during their working years and now in retirement, they volunteer at the local hospital as mentors for new nurses. Mentoring allows them to stay connected in their respective fields as well as provide a valuable service to the community.

RECONNECT

Have you ever wondered what people from your past (high school, college, business) are doing now? Remembering fun times from the past may pique your interest in reconnecting. Go ahead—do it. You might be very surprised.

The best way to try to reconnect with anyone seems to be through social media and wow—what an exciting feeling that can be when you do connect. You may once again be able to relive some of the fun times you had together and then be connected forevermore. You may even find you are able to meet in person.

A client of mine recounts an amazing story of reconnection. He attended school in New Orleans where his family lived at the time. His father was relocated, and he moved north with his family where he attended college and lost touch with all of his friends in New Orleans. When Hurricane Katrina hit New Orleans and left mass destruction, many of his friends from high school were affected. A fellow classmate began posting queries on Facebook asking for any information about his classmates. When my friend heard about this from another friend, he contacted the classmate immediately. As it turned out, many others from the same class also reconnected. Update emails began to flow to everyone in the class about the conditions after the hurricane, which needed help, and where everyone ended up. To this day, communication between the class members is active and many have met personally. My client now meets with a former classmate in Arizona hseveral times a year. Neither knew the other was nearby.

Family reunions can jump-start a reconnection with family members with whom you may have lost touch such as siblings, cousins, aunts, and uncles. Often, people relocate to many different parts of the country, and traveling can be difficult as well as expensive. The result is that you lose touch, and communication fades away. Why not plan a family reunion at a fun destination, and encourage everyone to attend? Bringing family back together can be very rewarding for everyone, especially you because you made it happen.

Estrangement among family members is not uncommon. Geographical situations or misunderstood events of the past can linger for years, or forever, if something doesn't happen to bring together family again.

Reconnection is a beautiful thing for the workaholic who never had time for his or her family. Any little time after work was spent with a nose in the briefcase until bedtime. Weekends were jam packed with back-to-the-office time to catch up. You lost yourself in corporate exuberance. There was very little time for family trips or just throwing the ball around. Retirement came and the shock set in. Maybe now you can work on finding the real you and bringing your family back together. You may be able to redeem yourself through reconnection with your loving family.

Reconnection can happen when attending school reunions. Many people shy away from these events due to the fear of being shocked by seeing changes in people and having people see changes in them. But there are many tales of reconnections by first loves who found that special moment again.

Retirement is a great time to reconnect with the joys of the past through old friends.

PICK UP YOUR OLD PASTIMES

Remember how you used to love bridge? You haven't played bridge for many years because you were so very busy with work and family. Now you have the time and there are bridge clubs in most towns. All it takes is reaching out and asking when is the next game and how you can get involved. This may become a regular date on your calendar now and you will most likely meet new people.

Maybe you always have had the desire to restore an old car. Now that you have the time, you can shop for a great deal on that classic car, and then take your time to restore it a little at a time. Most of the parts for classic cars are relatively inexpensive—especially if you are not worried about matching the VIN (vehicle identification number) for a rare 1957 Chevy Bel Air coupe.

Another client of mine has a 1966 El Camino that he bought when he was eighteen years old. He has kept it garaged for all these years. As he approaches retirement, gradually, he has been buying the parts he will need to restore it. The restoration process will begin once he is fully retired. This is an excellent non-financial retirement plan.

You may have told yourself that if you ever had the time you would go to museums and Broadway shows. You might even join a group that plans museum visits and lunches together every month. Why not join now? You have control over your own calendar. What other pastimes did you used to love to dream about? Is there any reason that you can't take up these pastimes again, or begin the one you always dreamed of doing? Now is the time to get outside of your comfort zone and get a little crazy. Come on—you know how much you always liked to dance, remember? There are so many programs available for seniors who want to get dancing again. If you search, *dancing for seniors* in your area on the Internet, you will be surprised at how many opportunities there are for you to get dancing again.

KEY NOTES FOR CHAPTER THREE

- Make new friends. Build relationships through social networks.
- Socialize. Doing so will energize and nourish you by increasing healthy habits such as exercise.
- Find ways to plan playdates for yourself with others. Set up bimonthly coffee dates or luncheons. Cook for others if you like.
- Fill up your calendar. Have a reason to get up every day and get out there.

CHAPTER 4

PLAY HARD, AND TAKE LEISURE IN MODERATION

"Just play. Have fun. Enjoy the Game."

—MICHAEL JORDAN, SIX TIME NBA CHAMPION

WHEN YOU WERE crazed and stressed at your job, you probably daydreamed about approaching retirement years. You lingered over those idyllic retirement advertisements that showed couples walking on the beach, golfing together, and dining over a moonlit bay with softly wafting breezes. Ah, you looked forward to the leisure life. Now that those idyllic days are here, you might be wondering what you will do with all of that leisure time, every day, for years to come—the endless vacation. The anticipation was so exciting, but now the reality of all your days filled with leisure has you thinking.

FIND THE BALANCE BETWEEN BODY AND MIND

An acquaintance of mine refers to herself as "ninety-four-years-young." She immersed herself in offering her "secrets to living a happy, healthy life" through bimonthly blogs. Her plan is to publish a book when she turns ninety-five. By then, she will have ninety-five secrets. She now has quite a following and works diligently at writing and distributing this valuable information. Her blogs are enlightening and encouraging and often quote research on topics such as the importance of daily exercise. This is her mantra: "You must want to live a long life and view living with grace and acceptance."

In one of her recent blogs, she shared the Centers for Disease Control and Prevention (CDC) recommendation that adults exercise at least one hour and fifteen minutes a week doing an aerobic physical activity on a vigorous level. She walks briskly at least one and a half miles each morning with her dog, and she practices exercises for thirty minutes at the end of each day. Her life is an excellent example of finding that balance between body and mind, and she has found a wonderful purpose for her retirement days.

Find that balance for you. If you love to take long walks every morning, maybe spend time in the afternoon volunteering at a library or reading the many books you never had time for in the past. For those who love the game of golf, now is the time to get out there in the sunshine and enjoy playing it. Golf can be a beautiful walk and a wonderful social time. When you return home after a good rousing game, relax and read a good book, or even join a book club as a mental balance to the physical sport.

There is another dimension to balance—mindfulness. Take some time every day to stop and listen, stop and feel.

Be here now. Don't think about tomorrow. Think about today, this minute. Appreciate the sounds of nature or that beautiful classical music playing on your radio. Close your eyes and allow yourself to breathe in the moment. As B.K.S. Iyengar—a famous yoga teacher—once said, "The rhythm of the body, the melody of the mind, and the harmony of the soul create the symphony of life."[6]

BE WILLING TO EVOLVE

Take time to reflect on and understand your personality traits that now fit in and complement your future. Are there changes you would like to make? Reinvent yourself and begin to redefine you. You may say that one of your traits that you will always be proud of is being independent even though you enjoy lively conversation with others once in a while.

You may not feel compelled to socialize with others often. But, in retirement, you will find that socialization was apparent every day at your job. You did not have to look for it as coworkers were always available, and you could choose to be independent or socialize. In retirement, you will find that you probably do not have this choice every day; you may find every day is empty of socialization unless you make it happen. You may want to consider evolving into someone who becomes more socially engaged. There is great importance in retirement to getting out there and socializing. Keep engaging with others and challenging your mind. Work at evolving into a more social person, and keep those communication skills sharp.

PLAY IS ACTIVE, LEISURE IS NOT

Be actively engaged in living. Get up, and get started—never mind sleeping late now. Life awaits—be there.

You may not realize that early morning hours can be refreshing, not stressful like you were used to when you had to get up, and get going before dawn. You can set your own pace now and plan your own day. You may find that getting up early gives you a whole day to plan.

Be active, not sedentary. Ditch the remote and think about what components will be essential to fulfilling your life now. There will be time for leisure, but get into activity, and play as much as possible. Try something new or get better at something old.

You may be thinking that you are tired and not in great physical shape after years of neglect to your body and poor eating habits brought about by stress and business travel. You may be thinking that activity sounds great, but you don't think it is for you. At this moment, you may be correct but with patience and dedication, you can begin to rebuild that endurance you did not know you still had. You may have to work hard to regain your physical well-being. Take one step today and maybe tomorrow; you will take two steps. Begin to become actively engaged little by little.

Don't be frustrated; take it one step at a time. If you have never played racquetball but have always wanted to give it a try, jumping right into a game might be a bit much. Yes, the sport is demanding, but with a lot of pre conditioning and addition of new flexibility into your life, you may be able to play this sport you have always wanted to play.

KEY NOTES FOR CHAPTER FOUR

- Find balance in your life between body and mind.
- A little leisure is OK but not too much. Be engaged actively in living now.
- Redefine you. Get to know the real you.
- Take it one step at a time, but keep moving forward.

CHAPTER 5

FLEXIBILITY IS POWERFUL

"Stay committed to your decisions, but stay flexible in your approach."

—TONY ROBBINS, MOTIVATIONAL SPEAKER

FLEXIBILITY IS DEFINED in three ways:

1. The ability to bend without breaking
2. The ability to be modified easily
3. The willingness to change or compromise

Wouldn't you agree that flexibility is a very powerful part of total wellness?

FLEXIBILITY FOR YOUR BODY

How does one maintain the flexibility of youth while aging? Several factors affect flexibility, including your genetic predisposition, your gender, and your body type.

Everyone's body is affected by age, including joint elasticity and muscle tendons. There is nothing more important related to flexibility than using your joints—or actually—exercise, itself.

Surely, you have heard the expression, "Use it or lose it." Flexibility affects your performance and will help you in the moment that you need it. If your body is limber, you will be more fluid and move more efficiently than a stiff body would move.

"Happiness is not a matter of intensity but of balance, order, rhythm and harmony."

THOMAS MERTON, AUTHOR

Amanda Allen, CrossFit coach says, "Do not go gently into the good night; life is always full of possibilities for accomplishment and change. Never tell me you're too old. Never tell me it's because you're aging that you are fat, sore, achy, can't recover, not as strong, not as fit, or...The list of excuses laid at the feet of aging is maddening and mistaken." Surely you get the point here. You must take personal responsibility for your own health and well-being, especially as you age. Be your own advocate for your overall wellness.

Researchers say that aging is a process that can be slowed, but it is your choice—it does not just happen. There are no magic pills; there are only daily choices, daily actions, and daily discipline.

Keep your nutrition pure. Choose what you put in your body, what you expose yourself to environmentally, how much sleep you get, how you hydrate yourself, and what exercise you practice daily.

Follow these guidelines:

1. Make movement a habit, not a chore. Sit less; walk more.
2. Do what comes naturally and what you enjoy. "Aha," you say you don't know yet what you really enjoy? Work on finding that. Embrace new challenges.
3. Lift things, that are within your ability.
4. When you feel like adding more to your workout, move faster.
5. Resting positions that help to improve movement include the following:
   a. **Squatting**. Ease into this position; it may be awkward at first.
   b. **Kneeling**. From kneeling, you can find the child's pose position a yoga position that helps to elongate your back.
   c. **Long sitting on the floor**. Sit with your legs extended in front of you, and try not to collapse down.

     d. **Cross-legged**. If you have always been a sitter and did minimum movement, you may find it difficult to have your legs in a low position. It may take some time to get your legs closer to the floor.

     e. **Side-sitting**. You will notice the difference in the flexibility in each hip.

6. To find some additional flexibility exercises recommended by the National Institute on Aging visit: https://www.nia.nih.gov/health/publication/exercise-physical-activity/sample-exercises-flexibility. (Additional resources can be found in the Appendix.)

You may ask how much and what types of exercise do you need to maintain and improve fitness? Several research studies [6] suggest that older individuals have a higher physical potential than what was believed many years ago. Safety continues to be the major concern with elder exercise programs.[7]

One important area is hydration because elderly individuals have a lower proportion of total body water. Water intake needs to be attended to seriously.

Before you embark on an exercise program, attainable goals need to be identified. The American College of Sports Medicine recommends exercise tolerance testing before elders begin a vigorous training program. [8] Your overall goals in your exercise program should be to improve cardiovascular endurance, strength, and flexibility. Maybe begin each day with a few stretching exercises and a nice long walk!

There is another side to getting involved in sports or even continuing the sports that are familiar to you. An acquaintance of mine has been a downhill skier for the past thirty years. She has loved every minute of this sport and spent her weekends as a ski instructor and even raised her sons in this sport. Skiing was actually a family lifestyle. As she aged, she began to lose some of her confidence, fearing that a fall might break something or injure her in another way. She became depressed over this view of her future and began to avoid winter sports completely until one day; a doctor mentioned to her that cross-country skiing was an excellent replacement for downhill skiing. She was not sure she would like this as it was mostly on flat ground and seemed to require great physical stamina. But she agreed to try the sport and when she did, she was amazed at how refreshed she felt and physically fit after only two hours. She was elated to have found a satisfying replacement for the downhill skiing that had been such a big part of her family life.

Here is the moral of this story: while you may have limitations as you age, you can redefine yourself in a similar manner that is more fitting for this time in your life. However, even cross-country skiing would not have been possible if she had not maintained flexibility as she aged.

FIND NEW FLEXIBILITY IN YOUR MIND-SET

Embrace new challenges. After all, seventy-five is the new fifty-five, isn't it?

After completing many mindfulness studies on aging, Harvard psychologist, Ellen Langer, reported that we are victims of our own stereotypes about aging and health. We accept those negative reminders about disease and old age—reminders that shape our self-concepts and our behavior. In one of her studies with a group of seventy- and eighty-year old men, she brought them to a location that reminded everyone of their lives twenty years earlier. The men were told to act as if they had traveled back in time, not to reminisce.

Langer's objective was to see if changing the men's mind-sets about their own ages might actually lead to changes in their health and fitness. The results were amazing. After one week, the men in the experimental group had more flexibility, increased dexterity, and less arthritis in their hands. Their mental acuity had risen significantly, and their gait and posture were much improved. Their aging process had in some measure been reversed.

What Langer suggested through her study results was that through some mindfulness, you might be able to embrace uncertainty and understand that the way you feel today may or may not connect to the way you feel tomorrow. If you are open to the idea that things can improve, you might wake up feeling younger.

Productive aging is a continued commitment to society through volunteerism and other forms of contribution that you do for you and for others. Being more successful and less static than merely aging successfully allows elders to maintain more positive and flexible outlooks in the face of obstacles. A flexible and positive mind-set is the key to successful aging.

"A flexible and positive mindset is the key to successful aging."

—Unknown

When you opt for retirement—whether complete retirement or partial retirement—opportunities and challenges abound, and many current retirees have changed their views on retirement already. In a study completed by the Association of Retired Persons (AARP)—comprising pre retirees—it was reported that 43 percent of participants are planning to engage in some sort of work after age sixty-five, and many are looking forward to changing careers in an effort to reduce stress or workloads. Some are interested in new experiences, and others plan to remain in their current career fields. The interesting take-away here is that almost 50 percent of new retirees plan to remain active and involved—not simply focused on leisure activities. These people look forward to a productive retirement.

You may be looking at twenty to thirty years in retirement and having a non-financial plan before you retire is definitely a good idea. There will be challenges along with the opportunities. Face these challenges that are on the retirement horizon with determination. You may have been a detailed planner in your past job. People depended on you to get things done and on time. Once you retire, the number of people who care if you get things done will be reduced dramatically. The result of this may be that you procrastinate now and don't really get the things done that you planned. You were a goal setter in business and now you only account to you.

What can you do to meet these challenges?

1. **Define your sense of purpose**. Whether you remain in your present career in some way, or you get into something new, fill up your calendar. Embrace this challenge.
2. **Have a reason to get up every day**. Whether you are looking at a four-hour commitment or an eight-hour commitment every day, get up and get going. Fill up your calendar. Embrace this challenge.
3. **Find that new pressure that pushes you**. You may find it easy to make excuses in order not to do something. Someone may drop in, relatives may decide to visit, or you may feel like sitting on the patio. Plow forward and don't be distracted. Protect your calendar. Embrace this challenge.
4. **Choose something that makes you smile or helps you feel more informed today than you were yesterday.** Set goals. Embrace this challenge.

5. **Maintain flexibility in your retirement mind-set**. Embrace this challenge.

FLEXIBILITY IN YOUR DAILY LIFE

You may have to remind yourself from time to time that retirement is not an event—it is an extended part of life and may include new careers, new forms of involvement in society, new relationships, and finally, the realization of postponed hopes and dreams. With all of this to look forward to, recasting your daily life to enjoy retirement may present a challenge. Finding that flexibility to achieve your new balance between purpose and leisure may not be easy. You lived your past life on a tight schedule that you have no longer.

"Retirement is not an event, it is an extended part of life."

—Unknown

Retirement is a good time to enjoy the opportunities that the Internet offers. You may never have spent time simply surfing the Internet, researching that recipe you always wanted to make or the golf vacation you promised yourself.

Or you may feel left out with the electronic progress of today and because of this, avoid any time with the Internet. You may not have a computer. Put this on your to-do list: buy a computer and take classes that help you master what you have feared. Even if you have decided to take up a new career or continue in your past career, you can find the time to learn how to enjoy the Internet. You will be amazed at the opportunities available on the Internet—local clubs to join, instructions for knitting that sweater you always wanted, upcoming events you might like to attend, social sites that might help you to reconnect with past acquaintances, and online courses. If you want to look into getting that advanced degree and you cannot make a commitment to leave your home, there are now many colleges and universities that offer that opportunity on line. (See the Appendix for references.)

You may be thinking that achieving more flexibility in daily life is not as easy as it sounds. "It might be easy for some, but not for me." You are correct, and you may have responsibilities as a caregiver, or you are anticipating this responsibility in the near future. As much as you would like to have a second career, you may not see how this will be possible. Finding that flexibility may be a challenge that you see as insurmountable; however, there are some things you should try to address:

- Protect your own wellness by getting physical exercise and maintaining good nutrition. Even a short walk daily can be a positive beginning.

- Find help with your daily responsibility—whether that person is a family member or another caretaker. Make time for you.
- Stay mentally healthy as well as physically healthy. Find that "you" time in every day.
- Take care of you, and that means seeking your time to do what you want.

Undoubtedly, the role of caretaker is one of the most demanding responsibilities in life and in retirement, this role can be completely overwhelming. There are times when the caretaker role is thankless and your mental state can be damaged severely. One of the greatest challenges you meet may be how to address your own needs when facing a daily responsibility of addressing someone else's needs.

Depression and physical exhaustion are common occurrences with full-time caretakers. Be protective of you. Find a way to take care of you—mentally and physically. Because this is such an important topic see chapter 8 for additional information regarding caretaking.

My mother is seventy-two years old, and her father (my grandfather)—who is ninety-three years old—is doing pretty well, physically. My client lives near her father and visits him frequently at his assisted living home; however, she hired a niece to oversee his daily needs outside of cooking and cleaning. The niece helps with his financial management and spends time with him, as well as taking care of other responsibilities. This type of help allows my mother to maintain her healthy retirement lifestyle routines as well as spend time with the rest of her family.

Caretaking assistance also allows my mother to spend more quality time with her father when she visits because she is not bogged down with taking care of his day-to-day responsibilities.

GET USED TO BEING RETIRED

At first, retirement may not live up to your expectations. You may still find it difficult to add more flexibility to your life and recast your days. Things have been the same day in and day out for so long, and now, all of a sudden, you don't have to put on that suit and run for the train.

Here are some ideas to think about for adding more flexibility into your daily life:

1. **You no longer have to awaken at 5:00 a.m. to fight that rush-hour traffic**. Change your wake-up time now to one that fits into your new schedule. Or keep the 5:00 a.m. wake-up time. Now put on your running shoes and take a nice, long early-morning walk or jog.

2. **Look at your calendar first thing when you awaken**. What's happening today? Do you have to get to a job? Do you need to get ready for a golfing date? Is there a special dinner to plan? Or is your morning free? Fill that free time with something special for you today. Plan a lunch, or meet friends for a hike.

3. **Maintain your mental flexibility**. If you have had a pattern of inflexibility, it may take some time to readjust your way of looking at things—especially in everyday situations. It might be tough to stay flexible if things

are not being done to your exacting standards. Try not to make your schedule too full on a daily/weekly/ monthly basis. You want to have time to go to the movies if a friend calls unexpectedly. Or you may want to be able to spend time with your grandkids from time to time. Look to chapter six for more guidelines on setting healthy boundaries in relationships.

4. **Find new incentives to help you to chill out**. Reward yourself with things that a make you feel special, such as back massages. How about a piece of dark chocolate now and again? Or maybe get your nails done, and how about a pedicure?

5. **Gaining mental flexibility is also a wellness goal for men as well as women**. If you have not been used to sharing your burdens with others, now is a good time to start. Learn to let go of that perfectionist bug.

6. **Stick to your exercise goals to maintain physical flexibility**. A study published in the 2012 Mayo Clinic Journal found that moderate exercise combined with computer use reduced the risk for memory impairment in people over seventy.[9] Here is proof that balancing physical and mental activities will provide the flexibility you reach for in retirement.

FIND FLEXIBILITY WITH YOUR THINGS

Flexibility with your things sounds impossible, doesn't it? But it is quite important if you think about it. Here is a good example of what might happen to you if you have decided to downsize and move to a two-bedroom condo. How are you supposed to move from a four-bedroom house complete with a den, basement, and an attic full of family keepsakes? You may have no intention of getting rid of all the family belongings and all your prized possessions and memories. The move looks good on paper, but when you actually think about moving to a much smaller place, you are pretty sure this will never work because you have too much stuff, and you will never get rid of your family memories.

Maybe it is time to think about your many things and whether you really want to move them with you. This idea will never work. It may be difficult, but you will have to think with strong flexibility about what you really need to take with you. All of those Halloween costumes your children wore throughout elementary school and the boxes of every drawing you children ever brought home to you are not essential to your lifestyle now.

Consider these guidelines:

- **Your children's belongings**: If your children do not want their games, easels, cars, truck, dolls, or erector sets, give them away to a charity where others can enjoy them.
- **Clothing**: You may have saved every beautiful three-piece suit you ever had, but you know deep down that you will never wear them again, especially because you plan to move south to warmer weather. There are many people who would love to have these suits. Give them away to a charity where others can use them.

- **The furniture:** This is a real challenge. You love that large sofa and loveseat. It took you years to find the perfect one, and now it will not fit where you are going. Let go of the furniture. Think about this as an opportunity to shop for new furniture. You may find you like the new furniture better than the old furniture. You may even get used to a queen-size bed instead of a king-size bed.

Think of yourself as becoming a minimalist. While this thought may not appeal to you, it may be a start to becoming more flexible with your things. If it is not necessary, part with it.

A friend of mine has always said, "It's not necessary." Shopping trips are simply for looking—never buying—in her opinion. She has enough, and she has always maintained this way of thinking. Her husband often teases her and reminds her that her headstone will read, "It's not necessary."

Even if you are not downsizing and simply remaining in your home, you may want to consider thinning out your stuff. Retirement is a good time to rethink why you have so many things—especially because you are planning to travel more. Do you really need to keep the old dollhouse and the dolls? What about your sugar cube or matchbook collection? Sugar is "out" in the nutrition department, and no one smokes anymore—at least, not in your house. What about your father's pipes and your mother's knitting needle collection? Is either of these pastimes on your radar? Think flexibility; think minimalist; think *less*.

But if you are a collector and have always looked forward to retirement as a time you might get involved seriously in collecting old glass, now is the time to be excited about this opportunity. Maybe you can research other collectors and events on the Internet to further enhance your interest. You may even decide to attend shows with other glass collectors. This is a great idea, but you can still become flexible with your other stuff and make room for your new collection.

Consider these guidelines:

- Get rid of duplicates.
- Make your home clutter-free.
- Travel lightly, pack lightweight clothes, and layer.
- Have fewer clothes. You no longer need seven different shirts or trousers.
- Simplify your meals.
- Determine what is enough for you, and get rid of the leftovers.

KEY NOTES FOR CHAPTER FIVE

- Make movement a habit, not a chore.
- Find a flexible, positive mind-set. Embrace new challenges.
- Recast your day. You no longer have to run for that train.
- Simplify your life.

CHAPTER 6

MAKE YOUR HEART SING

"Very little is needed to make a happy life; it is all within yourself, in your way of thinking."

—MARCUS AURELIUS, ROMAN EMPEROR

TAKE SOME TIME now and really learn about yourself. Learn about you. What lights your fire? Here are a few things to think about now that you are retired and you can spend time on you:

1. **Honor your body.** Be thankful for all that it does, and give it what it needs, like lots of exercise, hot showers, and lots of hydration. Make a list of everything you need to take care of yourself to feel healthy and grounded. Make your needs your number-one priority.
2. **Keep your mind full of positive thoughts.** Learn new things. Travel to new places. Find your passion in those positive thoughts.
3. **Do what you love.** Love who you are.

4. **Find that inner peace**. Every moment of life contains possibilities.
5. **Let your spirit soar**. Laugh a lot and see the world through those younger eyes. Nurture your spirit through a walk on the beach or just relaxing. Just be.
6. **Be beautiful**. Be you.
7. **Simplify your life**.
8. **Be happy in your skin**.

SPEND LESS TIME AND MONEY ON THINGS THAT DON'T MATTER

Now that you are retired, you can spend some time thinking about what really matters in your life. You have probably spent most of your career years working hard to please others. Now is the time to determine where you want to spend your time and your money.

The minimalist concept is actually a good place to start. Do you really need that third TV in your new condo or even in your house? You are retired now, and you are going to get out there and get involved. You are not going to stay home watching TV. Lose that remote because you are now going to spend less time doing things that do not matter. Don't buy that third TV. Instead, play more golf, take a computer lesson, or upgrade your computer. Maybe take a continuing education course at your local adult school or on line. Maybe spend that extra money on a nice vacation and consider splurging every once in a while and take the grandkids to someplace you have always wanted to go or someplace they have always wanted to go.

The best message here is to do what makes you happy—keep working, maybe not at your old career but in a new purpose. Find that purpose and spend your time and maybe your money there. Tangible things will not fill that purpose in your life, but new business cards or more education just might help you find your new passion.

An acquaintance who recently retired spends her day fretting about all her free time and regretting that she ever retired. She thought retirement would be full of exciting opportunities and that she would be very busy. But she has not left the house to meet those opportunities. She was a graphic artist in her career for many years and did a great job for the corporation. When she was offered an opportunity to retire, she took the offer immediately thinking retirement would be great.

She did no planning for her days ahead in retirement. What she might have done was to suggest to her company that she would be available for part-time or contract work, but she did neither. Friends have recently suggested to her that she print some business cards to give out to local businesses or advertise her skill and availability on the Internet. At the moment, she is not interested in what appears to be a struggle. Instead, she remains at home becoming more and more of a recluse. Many friends have attempted to include her in social events but she either comes and is very down or does not come at all. This is an unfortunate situation that is destined to destroy her wellness and sap her joy in retirement. The push to get her moving and out there now has to come from her; friends can no longer offer guidance.

Plan your retirement one step at a time. Find that purpose in your life—spend time on what really matters to you. Retirement can last another twenty to thirty years. Don't try to plan all twenty to thirty years at one time, maybe think about the next two years. Then, in two years, think about the next two years. The constant here is to do what makes you happy. Make your heart sing.

FAMILY TIME MATTERS, BUT SET THOSE BOUNDARIES

One of the very first things to remember in retirement is that the consequences of your retirement-planning decisions can affect more people than simply you and your spouse or partner. These decisions can impact your extended family and even your close friends in many ways. Should retirement be a family affair or something that you and your wife or partner decides jointly? If you do not include your family in your retirement planning, you may find some unhappiness in the results.

Maybe you have decided to move to a condo in another town or even an assisted-living facility on a golf course. Doing either of these things will no doubt remove you from immediate family or close friends. Your reasoning was simple— you and your wife or partner did not want to be a burden on your family as you aged. But is removing yourself completely from family the answer?

Or you may be removing yourselves from a constant babysitting situation. You may feel it is best to live far away so you do not have to feel guilty or resent the constant intrusion. But is it an intrusion, or is this something you can deal with by setting boundaries? On one hand, your children are probably thrilled that you will now have more time to spend with the grandchildren, or maybe they simply see you as an entitlement. Either way, this is a situation you should face head on. Set those boundaries—don't move out of town.

While most of us can agree that Grandchildren are a joy, you may want your time with them to be limited. After all, you and your spouse or partner retired so you could spend time together, not babysitting. Sit down with your family and tell them how you feel, and set those boundaries. Let them know that you have plans for retirement and when time allows, you will be happy to help out but not on a regular basis. If you do want to help out on a regular basis when you retire, and can't wait to spend every minute you can with your grandchildren, then by all means—make that your retirement plan.

While evaluating how you want to spend your time remember to take into consideration a couple of things: First depending on your family situation additional quality time with the grandkids could be very impactful on their lives. You now have the time to spontaneously take a grandkid out for ice cream or even take a small vacation just with grandkids. If you don't have grandkids look into local organizations that serve troubled or underserved children, like Big Brothers Big Sisters. Second meet with your financial advisor and really evaluate your financial situation and determine if you have sufficient money to splurge a little with your family or even personally. Do you want your kids to enjoy your money once you pass away or would you rather see them enjoy it while you are still alive? This is obviously a personal decision and there are many factors that go into it and like I said you need to meet with your advisor to determine if these things are possible. I have seen many clients save for their whole lives, and then have a little bit of a mental block when it comes to spending their money. It is as if it is engrained in their DNA to save but not to spend. It is definitely a balancing act but I have never seen a hearse with a luggage rack so re-evaluate your financial situation with your advisor to determine if you possibly could be spending more while you are alive and healthy. Some of my best memories as a kid are spending time with my grandparents. I remember my grandpa taking us to the state fair every year and it was always his treat to the family. While the financial outlay for this I am sure was not tremendous it still wasn't cheap and was not something that was in the budget for my parents at that time, the money spent however did create memories that I will have for the rest of my life.

Whatever your retirement plans, I cannot say enough about setting those healthy boundaries. Your children may want to travel occasionally without their children and would like to you to babysit if you are open to this sort of commitment. Let them know your comfort level up front and what you are not comfortable with. Be open with your family about your comfort or discomfort with frequency and length of the types of trips that will leave you in charge of your grandchildren. Remember that you are not going to get any younger, so do what you can with your grandchildren while your health is still with you.

Try not to give up family time and remove yourself completely; work it out by involving family in your retirement plans. Let family and friends know that you are excited about your retirement plans and hope they are happy for you. If you get any pushback from family, be firm in your approach and commitment to enjoy your retirement in the way you want to, but stay close if at all possible.

A client of mine retired recently, and part of her long-term retirement plan was to move closer to her son so that she could care for her grandchildren on a daily basis. While this plan may not be everyone's idea of good retirement, the plan was exactly what she wanted, and today she is very happy with her retirement life.

KEY NOTES FOR CHAPTER SIX

- Make your heart sing; find that passion that makes you smile.
- Plan your retirement one piece at a time; look two years ahead, not twenty years ahead.
- Be open with your family and friends when you plan retirement.
- Relish your family time, but set healthy boundaries to protect what you want in retirement.

CHAPTER 7

RELATIONSHIPS: THE BALANCING ACT

"Retirement has been a discovery of beauty for me.
I never had the time before to notice the beauty of
my grandkids, my wife, the tree outside my very
own front door and, the beauty of time itself. "

—HARTMAN JULE,, ADVERTISING EXECUTIVE

THE BEST NON-FINANCIAL retirement advice I can offer you is to take time to adjust to being retired. Don't try to do everything you planned right away. Be patient with your spouse or partner. If you want to sleep late, and your spouse wants to begin early morning walks—so be it. Learn to express yourself if your spouse wants to do something that you do not want to do.

Retirement is a major change and very often, change is stressful. Ending a career is a major lifestyle transition and not always a happy one. Couples must acknowledge the fact that marriage will be different in retirement. Recognize that you are going through a major life transition.

COMMUNICATE OFTEN

Communication is critical to help adapt to each other's new schedules and retirement lifestyles. One of you may still be working and expectations about house chores can cause conflict. Retirement will force you to change the way you interact with your spouse. Without the daily challenge of running a business, you may find you are becoming more controlling with your spouse. This will most likely cause conflict. Begin to adapt to your new relationship by opening the lines of communication. Relearn how to relate to each other. Be each other's best friend, and make an honest commitment to each other. Share your desires to be a part of each other's life always, but respect each other's space. Share your interests, but respect each other's separate interests and need to have time alone.

Spend time laughing every day! Always listen to each other and see each other's point of view. While you may have separate interests or continue part-time employment or mentoring, you can still share a community involvement such as church or a community charitable organization.

Talk about the future. The future in retirement may include illness or other physical neediness. At some point, the future will include death. Keep things positive but always in perspective. Even though you will respect each other's individual interests, you should try to do as much together as possible. That being said can there be too much togetherness? Absolutely, twenty-four hours a day together can be too much. Talk about how retirement will affect your relationship before retirement.

DON'T BE AFRAID TO GO TO A COUNSELOR

As you transition to a completely new stage in your marriage, inevitably, there will be unexpected changes and challenges. One way to deal with these challenges is to see a counselor. However, for many people over the age fifty, the thought of seeing a counselor seems to be very intimidating. It may even be so intimidating that they would rather live retirement in a very unhealthy/unhappy marriage than go to see a counselor.

A study in the *Journal of Counseling & Development* in 2007 says that less than one-third of individuals who experience psychological distress seek help from a mental health professional. The same study says that there are five avoidance factors in the help-seeking process:

1. Social stigma
2. Treatment fears (what will they have me do?)
3. Fear of showing and feeling emotions
4. Anticipated utility and risks (is it going to be worth my time?)
5. Self-disclosure (being vulnerable)

While each of these factors is valid and can be considered a good justification for not seeing a counselor, they should instead be acknowledged so that you can then overcome the factor and seek counseling as needed. A few sessions of being in an uncomfortable situation could translate to a far healthier and happier retirement.

Just like it would have probably been a good idea for every engaged couple to seek some counseling before getting married, it is probably even better counsel to seek counseling in retirement. Now you have the time and likely the money to be able to do so. This could even be done on a *proactive* rather than *reactive* basis—in other words, don't wait until you have marriage problems to seek some professional help.

Everyone's marriage—no matter where it is currently—can always be improved upon. I have a two friends that are marriage counselors and they both have told me that they really wish people would come to them at the very beginning stages of marital problems instead of waiting until they are on the brink of divorce and are mentally checked out. They say that even better than that would be to come to them with the goal of turning a "good" marriage into a "great" marriage. Think of it like getting your car serviced—if you were to drive a car for a hundred thousand miles and never changed the oil or got it serviced, you would likely ruin the engine beyond repair. The same goes for your marriage.

One last thought on this topic. Just like any other profession, there are good and bad counselors; put in the work to find one you like. It may require meeting with a few before you find one who feels comfortable to both of you.

STAKE YOUR SPACE

Some research reports that men assume their wives will be totally focused on them in retirement. Women, on the other hand, might become resentful or angry if they have to give up more personal time. This thinking is not realistic or healthy; however, communication can help to ease expectations.

Pursue your own interests and maintain some separate friendships. In addition to allowing space, your goals and friendships offer opportunities for your own personal growth and help you to maintain your unique identity. In addition to ensuring your emotional well-being, time spent apart will give you something to talk about when you are together.

Establish separate spaces in your home for each of you. Probably, you have your own pursuits and/or hobbies and definitely, you need your own space to pursue them. Whether it is an office with a computer or an art studio, make sure each of you has your own "space." Individual space will keep both of you from feeling as though you are intruding or being intruded upon. Yes, it is important to spend time together, but it is just as important to spend time alone.

MAKE ROOM FOR EACH OTHER'S IDEAS, AND LEARN TO COMPROMISE

You may want to move to a condo closer to your son, but your spouse has dreams of living on a lake so he can fish every day. These ideas are seemingly far apart and finding a compromise here appears unlikely. But maybe a halfway point can be found by discussing each of your dreams for relocating. A condo near your son may sound wonderful as you are hoping to spend more time with the grandkids; however, your spouse does not have the same desire. He has always looked forward to spending more time fishing—something he loves but never had much time to do when he was working. He really does not want to spend his days babysitting his grandkids. He is fine with seeing them once in a while, but not on a regular basis.

Maybe through discussion and appreciation for each other's desires, you can come to a compromise where each of you is happy. What if you found a condo halfway between the lake and your son's home? Or what if you gave up seeing your grandkids on three days a week, and you went to the lake with your spouse so he could fish? Maybe a compromise by each of you would offer a solution.

Neither of you will have everything your way 100 percent of the time, but compromising will offer each of you a chance to do what you have been looking forward to in retirement. Many of your decisions will be based on your financial situation, so you may have to sharpen your pencils to see how each of you can be accommodated. One of you may need a part-time job to afford a specific type of lifestyle. Sit down and talk, and then talk some more. Eventually, you will reach that space where you both agree on where and how you will live in retirement.

Retirement is not a one-way street; encourage each other to be happy in retirement.

Here are a few pointers to help keep your relationship healthy:

1. **Don't let yourself go**. Both of you must take pride in how you look. Keep fit and healthy so you can enjoy your retirement years together.
2. **Set boundaries with your children**. Do you both agree with daily babysitting so your children can return to work, or do you both want more independence so you can do more in the community or travel more?
3. **Remember, it is not all about you**. Compromise, compromise, compromise. Come up with that dream together.
4. **Nurture your relationship**. Communication, loyalty, and respect make up the foundation of a strong, enduring relationship.
5. **Talk about new possibilities**. Try something new together.

BOOMERANG CHILDREN

If you have a child who has returned to live with you—probably for financial reasons—you have a "boomerang" child. Usually, this situation is not planned for when you and your spouse or partner discuss retirement. But your child needs you now, and probably, you cannot say *no*. Mounting credit-card and student-loan debt have made it impossible for your son or daughter to afford to rent an apartment even with a job.

A recent study by *Age Wave* reported that one in five parents age fifty and older has as least one boomerang, adult child who has moved back home.[10] According to Pew Research Center, more than twenty-six million young adults now live with their parents—the highest level in more than forty years.[11] Considering this potential jolt to your retirement plans, what can you do to smooth this transition?

- Communication is key to helping your adult child understand the changes you have gone through since he or she moved out. Maintain an open dialogue to avoid misunderstandings.
- Set ground rules—after all, you are now retired and have plans.
- Set goals for when that child will move out. In almost every scenario, it is going to be far better for both parties to have their own spaces again, eventually.

SINGLE IN RETIREMENT

More and more folks are delaying or forgoing marriage completely. A new generation is approaching retirement single. Researcher, Eric Klinenberg, spent many years gathering statistics that show a very large change in the way we now live. In 1950, only 9 percent of Americans lived alone. Now, more than half of Americans are single, and more than half of those people live alone making up almost 30 percent of households.

Klinenberg also reported that most folks who live alone are not isolated but very involved socially and in other ways. For those who did not enter retirement solo, being newly single in retirement can be the result of divorce or widowhood.

There is no question that "singlehood" in retirement comes with its challenges. Research shows that a single, retired person tends to save less for retirement than a married couple. If there is a financial setback or an unexpected emergency, there is only one person to cover costs. However, on the flip side, a single person can invest, budget, and spend as he or she sees fit. There is no need to compromise or accept another person's disagreeable approach to money management.

Another challenge to retiring single is avoiding isolation and making new connections after work. Retired couples tend to encourage each other to do new things and go places. Solo retirees must push themselves to get out on their own. There is no ready-made community now and sometimes singles fear loneliness. However, by building a network of friends slowly, single retirees can stay in the game.

You have to put yourself out there and get engaged in something in order to meet people. Find something you like to do and find a way to do it. A client of mine did just that after his wife died instantly of a heart attack. He had recently retired and was devastated because they had just begun to build a wonderful, active life together for retirement. He always loved to ski and decided to become a part time ski instructor at a ski resort a few hours away to keep busy. It would allow him free skiing for the season and provide opportunities to meet new people. About a year after her death he ended up meeting somebody new at the ski resort who shared a lot of his hobbies.

This was several years ago that they got married and every time I see him and now her they seem to be doing great and are always talking about their next action packed excursion they are going on. Despite dealing with the unexpected loss of his wife early in retirement, his retirement years can still be beautiful and perfect because he pursued his passion.

"Find something you like to do, and find a way to do it."

—Unknown

YOU MET SOMEONE—ARE YOU READY TO REMARRY?

Divorce or death of a spouse is inevitable for retirees, and finding love or companionship is actually quite common in retirement. Here are a few thoughts on what you should think about before remarrying:

- **Finances**: Be transparent about money. Sit down and talk about finances. This now includes pension, savings, emergency funds, and investments outside of savings. Expenses and debts must be transparent—so must your credit report because this tells the story of how well you manage your finances.
- **Important documents**: You may have prepared these long ago, and now they need updating to include your new life.
- **Prenuptial agreement**: Separate your finances prior to entering into another marriage. This protects children on both sides.
- **Your own self-esteem**: Unemployment brings poor self-esteem. Sometimes, folks feel there is nothing they can do about how they feel and the fact they now have a big emptiness where they always had a job.
- **Health**: As you age, your health may deteriorate, and large expenses may loom ahead. How will you manage this part of your new marriage? Look into long-term-care insurance.
- **Merging lifestyles**: Over the years, you both became set in your ways. How will you manage to merge two very different lifestyles? Constant communication about this topic is advisable before your remarry.

- **Remarriage (does it make financial sense?):** Consult your CPA and lawyer with this question as things like Social Security, estate planning, and long-term insurance needs may be affected.

MANAGING YOUR EXTENDED FAMILY IN RETIREMENT

Retirement is becoming a family affair these days. Family will make your life in retirement a lot more enjoyable because most of you will now have the time to enjoy your adult children, grandchildren—and maybe other relatives you have not seen in a very long time. But with all of the enjoyment, rising longevity is requiring today's pre-retirees to focus outside of themselves and support their parents emotionally, physically, and even financially. In addition, adult children and other younger relatives may be struggling with inadequate careers and financial difficulties causing them to turn to their parents—you. Parenthood does not retire.

Most pre-retirees age fifty and over have never prepared for providing support—especially financial—to other family members. Pre-retirees have pretty much focused on putting aside a nest egg for themselves and talking about what they would like to do in retirement.

Other challenges in retirement can occur in blended families as part of extended families. Because of the rising divorce rates of the 1980s, two in five people over the age of fifty are now part of a blended family including stepsiblings, stepchildren, and/or stepparents. Blended families not only create financial challenges, but also emotional challenges for both parents and siblings.

Ongoing family communication that stays on track proactively may help you and your spouse to enjoy a more stress-free retirement. In many cases, families find open discussions about family challenges uncomfortable and in some cases, there is great fear of family conflict.

Here are a few ideas to think about for your family communications:

- **Plan ahead for potential family challenges**. Yes, there are many important financial topics such as net worth, long-term care, where to live in retirement, and inheritance plans that probably you will discuss. However, there are non-financial issues to discuss as well.
- **Make a family plan**. How will you be cared for as you age? Will you want to remain in your home with a caretaker, move in with your adult children, or move to an assisted-living center where all of your needs will be met? This may be an uncomfortable topic, but planning ahead will avoid difficulties and bad decision-making later.
- **Talk early and talk often with all family members**. Your family meetings should include all members of your extended family.

Recently, an acquaintance of mine relayed a sad story about her parents who had just passed away. The daughter decided to move her parents into her home in Southern California where they could enjoy warmer temperatures and have her close by. The home had an unattached garden apartment with a patio and seemed perfect for her parents. The daughter was available, and they saw each other daily. The mother died after living there for several years, but the daughter was happy that her last days were peaceful. Her father became angrier at life each day and insisted on his own independence except his need for her to shop for him. Although she offered to help with financial management, he refused to share any information at all with her, including his investments, financial worth, or any other matters.

After some time, he needed a live-in caretaker, which my friend found for him. Throughout his remaining days, he refused to share any financial or other important information with my friend. When he died, my friend was left with trying to figure out where his assets were and how she should manage everything. She discovered that he had given most of his cash assets to his caretaker. While this is a sad story, it is a good example of how living boundaries should be set up front with multigenerational families who decide to live together and how ongoing communication might help. If my friend had discussed her concern for future needs with her parents before they moved in, there might have been a plan for her to help with financial management.

KEY NOTES FOR CHAPTER SEVEN

- Communication is the beginning of all understanding. Communicate often.
- Learn how to listen to each other. Learn how to compromise.
- Be patient in retirement. You are beginning a very important lifestyle transition.
- Today, retirement is a family affair—not just an individual consideration. Hold ongoing family meetings to discuss your retirement and challenges ahead.
- Don't be afraid to see a counselor even if you don't think your marriage is broken.

CHAPTER 8

OTHERS AND OTHER THINGS TO CONSIDER

CREATE A HOME FOR YOUR CHANGING NEEDS

As you age, you will probably see signs that you are not as spry as you were once. Staying in a home with three stories and many steps is probably not a good idea, and addressing this issue is most likely something you want to avoid because you love your house. Recognize that your needs will change as you age. I recently visited a widow in her beautiful two story home on the lake, she mentioned that for the last several years she has been living only on the first floor (the master bedroom is upstairs). While this has worked for a while she is now deciding to sell and move to a one story home. In her situation there was no financial need to move to a smaller home but in some cases downsizing could be something that helps you transition into retirement even faster. That being said, I have other clients that prefer to stay in a larger home so as to have room to accommodate guests and kids as they come back to visit. As you can see there is no right answer for everyone the point is to take make sure you have considered all the pros cons and make the best decision for you and your family.

CAREGIVING OF SOME SORT IS LIKELY

Finding a way to have a home on one level is ideal. If you can reconfigure your current home to do this, fine, but if that isn't a viable option, think about moving to a home that fulfills this need. The day may come when you or your spouse or aging parent needs a wheelchair or a walker, and steps will be a hindrance.

Most likely, you and/or your spouse will become a caregiver in the future. This might be for a spouse but could also be for a parent. Like previously mentioned boundaries are important when deciding what is best for aging parents; however remember that the parent that needs your help is the same parent that raised you. This does not mean that you need to drop everything and become a fulltime caregiver of your parents but it does mean that you might have to adjust your retirement schedule to accommodate their needs. In many cultures multigenerational homes are very common. It is definitely less common in the United States, but still could be a scenario that could realistically be something you may want or need to consider. These experiences can be wonderful learning and growing opportunities for everyone involved if they are taken on with the right attitude.

CAREGIVING CAN BE REWARDING

Multigenerational could also mean living with and/or raising grandchildren. Studies show that approximately 7% of children are raised by grandparents. This isn't necessarily something you can plan on or should necessarily plan on, I simply mention it so that it is something you can be aware of so that if it does happen it does not catch you off guard. I have 3 different clients that each are raising grandkids for one reason or another. Each of them embrace it wholeheartedly and have never complained about it once. That doesn't mean it is easy but most things that are worthwhile are not easy. While they are aware that it is going to be a drastically different retirement picture than what they originally pictured it is still a very beautiful picture.

As you consider the possibilities of caring for others whether it be a spouse, a parent or a grandchild here are a few things to take into consideration:

- **Caregivers have less time for other family members and themselves**. In a recent study by National Alliance for Caregiving and AARP, more than half of caregivers reported that their duties have caused them to sacrifice vacations, hobbies, or other activities.[12]

- **Balancing work and caregiving**. Many caregivers ask managers in their workplaces to allow them to change their work times to accommodate their needs. In most cases if you openly communicate with managers and coworkers they are happy to accommodate.

- **Do not always think of it as a burden**. While it is most definitely going to be a paradigm shift as far your schedule goes, it can provide amazing opportunities for you to learn things as well as those around you. It can help you serve and can help you be an example of service to those around you.

- **Physical and mental stress**. Providing intense care for long periods can cause heavy physical and mental tolls. Caregivers report that frustration, exhaustion, anger, and sadness are often a result of caretaking.

Sometimes, a debilitating disease can change hopes and dreams for the future. Shock, disbelief, and denial can take place as you are caught off guard. Another painful adjustment for caregivers is coping with changes in the patient's personality. When the patient is in pain or having a bad day, the caregiver is subjected to irritability, anger, temper outbursts, and mood swings. Caregivers often experience feelings of isolation and not being appreciated, emotional and physical exhaustion, and being mentally drained. Keeping up the demands of caretaking takes its toll. Make sure you take care of you. Make time for yourself both mentally and physically, find a way to get a way periodically to recharge.

You may have high expectations for yourself or your spouse as a caretaker—you may try to do too much and feel guilty when you cannot manage. Coming to the realization that being strong as a caretaker does not mean doing it alone will help you cope. Share the care and ask others for help. Take better care of yourself to cope with the demands of caretaking. Give yourself permission to be just a human being. As you make these decisions about how to care for others and how much you should do versus having others do, make sure you make those decisions after much thought, prayer and soul searching, and remember to think about the positive aspects of caring for others.

KEY NOTES FOR CHAPTER EIGHT

- There are many different types of caretaking.
- Caretaking no matter what the scenario is going to require sacrifice.
- Caretaking should not always be seen as a burden.

CHAPTER 9

YOUR LEGACY

The greatest legacy one can pass on to one's children and grandchildren is not money or other material things accumulated in one's life, but rather a legacy of character and faith.

—BILLY GRAHAM, AMERICAN EVANGELIST

THE WORD, *LEGACY,* usually describes the property that people leave their heirs when they die. But there is a non-material legacy that you will leave behind that is far more important than your material wealth—a lifetime of relationships, accomplishments, truths and value, and the lives you touched during your lifetime.

Recent research reports that as people age, they continue to face important developmental milestones. Learning and emotional growth do not stop during aging—they continue through many deep and sustaining opportunities.

Physician and gerontologist, Gene Cohen, MD, says, "Older people are driven by an urgent desire to find larger meaning in the story of their lives through a process of review, summarizing, and giving back." Recognizing someone's legacy will allow others to understand that person better and appreciate him or her more.

Have you given some thought to your legacy and what you might like people to know about your life well lived? The legacy of your life is a unique expression of your relationship with others including siblings, your spouse, children, grandchildren, neighbors, friends, and maybe even pets. If you should become incapacitated, how would this affect them? What if you could no longer make decisions that affect your own life and their lives? What would you want to say to these individuals if you had one more chance to speak to them directly?

How might the legacy of your life create more opportunities or higher aspirations for them?

Look inward at your values and then outward at how they have manifested in the achievements of your life. Is it important to know that you have made a difference in the world? What are the accomplishments that you are most proud of? Has your charitable giving made a difference or contributed to your family's accomplishments? What do you want to be your legacy?

Write your "Love Letter Legacy" (found in the appendix)—a legacy for the living that is a gift of love, values, belief, wisdom, and clarity.

> *"Life can only be understood backward; but it must be lived forward."*

> —SOREN KIERKEGAARD (DANISH PHILOSOPHER)

LOVE LETTER LEGACY

Everyone leaves a legacy, but you can leave a legacy of information and avoid a legacy of confusion. A Love Letter Legacy is sometimes referred to an "ethical will." It is a non-binding document that may or may not accompany a more strictly structured legal document. Each Love Letter is as unique as the person writing it. There is no right or wrong way to write a Love Letter Legacy. (See the Appendix for a sample Love Letter Legacy.)

If a Love Letter Legacy is not legally binding, why should you prepare one? A Love Letter Legacy is an opportunity for you to tell your life story, talk about the experiences that shaped your personality, and communicate from the position of thoughtful reflection. Your Love Letter will serve a number of purposes:

- Writing down your values and beliefs will also help crystallize them for you. You may learn a lot about yourself in the process.
- Telling your family what matters most to you and what you hope will matter to them. This can help you to come to terms with your own mortality.
- Asking for forgiveness and forgiving. This is a way for you to say what you have not been able to say before to a person directly.
- Striking the right tone in what you write. Don't blame or bring up old conflicts.
- Spelling out clearly what you want to happen to your assets after you are gone. You will be leaving behind

much more than material things. Your values, spiritual beliefs, wisdom, hopes for your descendants, and love you feel for family and friends are all intangibles that may represent the greatest gifts you can leave for loved ones.

A Love Letter Legacy can be a gift that your loved ones did not even know they were looking for and can be the most priceless one they have ever received. In addition to the Love Letter Legacy—which can be short and to the point—why not begin writing your life story? You can put aside a short time every day, and write a bit as you remember important events from your past. You can also add a few chuckles that your loved ones might enjoy. You might have a good time with this project!

GET STARTED CRAFTING YOUR LIFE STORY

"Oh boy," you say. "I don't have the slightest idea of how to tell my life story, and no one would be interested anyway." On the contrary—your children and grandchildren might be very interested in your life story. After all, you are a big part of their lives.

Here are a few suggestions to get you started:

1. **Talk about your past**. Maybe include a special moment that connects you to today that happened to you when you were thirteen years old.
2. **Connect your life story**. Make it relevant to all the people you will share this story with.

3. **Include interesting childhood lessons**. Talk about some of the ones you learned from your grandparents, uncles, parents, teachers, and others. What did you learn that you pulled from throughout your life or even reflect on today?
4. **Keep it short**. No one wants to read page after page of every minute of your life.
5. **Blow your own horn**. You were a great leader in your career and you definitely left a legacy—you were a tough act to follow. Talk about that and tell everyone why you were so great at your job.
6. **Apply your success**. Show how it is part of your retirement.
7. **Share stories**. Tell about all parts of your life that you may be talking about for the first time.
8. **Get started now**!

KEY NOTES FOR CHAPTER NINE

- What do you want to be your legacy? Think about this.
- Leave a legacy of information—not one of confusion.
- Begin writing your Love Letter Legacy.

CHAPTER 10

A LAST WORD

*"Instead of saving for someone else's college educa-
tion, I'm currently saving for a luxury retirement
community replete with golf carts and handsome
young male nurses who love butterscotch."*

—JEN KIRKMAN

I LOVE THIS quotation by Jen Kirkman, one of our funniest
comedians. Her positive outlook on retirement makes one
smile, and it really does sound like a great plan. Of course,
not everyone would want this plan but maybe something like
it—maybe with chocolate instead of butterscotch. Why not
have a plan like this if you want? Sure, you have to be con-
servative with spending, but maybe—just maybe—there is
something like this, especially if you love golf.

When my clients ask me how to begin a Non-Financial
Retirement Plan, I tell them to begin with a blank canvas or
piece of paper. Get out a paintbrush or a pencil, and begin to
draw what you think retirement should look like for you. You

would be surprised at how many of my clients draw a lake with a dock. Very few draw a sandy beach or a golf course, even though the retirement commercials usually show beaches of golf courses. When I see the pictures with a lake and dock, I ask them how they picture themselves there and what they plan to do every day. Very few have an answer to that query. So what I deduce from this is that they picture peace, serenity, quietness, and an uncrowded community. I don't see other people in their pictures, and I don't see any activity.

While the lake idea seems idyllic, the truth is that after several weeks when the honeymoon is over, they will probably look at each other and say, "Is this all there is?" Retirement in today's world needs to be complete with friends, social activities, physical exercise, and most of all, mentally challenging activities on a daily basis.

Throughout this book, you have read about finding a purpose in your retirement life. Finding that daily reason to get up and get going. Sitting on a dock overlooking a lake every day will not survive your need to be valued in your life—a retirement life that could last twenty or thirty more years. You need to have a purpose in your life; you need a new career. You need to get a new canvas and a paintbrush, and begin again. This time, think about everything discussed in this book and begin the picture with a drawing of you.

I would like to leave you with a few questions to think about before you retire—before you put pencil to paper and begin writing your Non-Financial Retirement Plan.

QUESTION 1: SO WHERE DO YOU WANT TO LIVE WHEN YOU RETIRE?

Really, if you had no barriers—financial or otherwise—where would you like to live? This question may be very revealing to you and there may be a way you can come close to your dream. Don't be too hasty in putting this dream in a drawer; think about it for a bit, and revisit your ideas after you do some long thinking and discussing with your spouse and other family members. For some, the motor home sounds intimidating and the second home sounds overwhelming or not financially possible. Instead, each year pick a different destination in the country. Then, get on the website, VRBO.com, and rent a house for one month out of the year. Experience lots of new people and places with very little financial outlay.

QUESTION 2: WHAT DO YOU PLAN TO DO EVERY DAY DURING RETIREMENT?

You may be thinking that you will just go with the flow and see what happens. I encourage you to try to put a Non-Financial Retirement Plan in place before you retire. Have you thought about continuing your career in a different manner or becoming a mentor? Have you thought about looking in a new direction for a job or maybe continuing your education? Maybe you decided that you would become a volunteer with the school system.

QUESTION 3: HAVE YOU AND YOUR SPOUSE HAD A FAMILY MEETING TO DISCUSS YOUR RETIREMENT PLANS?

Today, retirement is a family affair as discussed in the relationship chapter. You and your spouse may have a plan, but do take time to bring your extended family members in on your plans. This is important especially if you have been supporting any other family members. Also, if you have adult children living with you, how will they manage once you are retired, or are you planning on living in your current home with them?

THE LAST WORD

There is so much to think about in a very busy life today. Many folks have adult children or other extended family members living with them, and it may seem impossible when you and your spouse think about making your own retirement plans. Don't be discouraged, communicate with your family, and let them know what you would like your retirement to look like. They may have plans for you, but this is your life, your retirement. Let everyone know what you want and how you want to do it. Whatever you decide, wherever you go, make your heart sing.

"And in the end, it's not the years in your life that count, it is the life in your years."

—Abraham Lincoln – Sixteenth President of the U.S.A.

I hope sincerely that this book has given you many things to think about as you embark on your new life stage of retirement. The transition can be challenging at times, but the end result will be well worthwhile. You and your spouse or partner will realize another twenty or thirty years embarking on new adventures. Try not to be impatient with yourself as you work to understand "you" and find true passion in your retirement.

If you have questions for me in the future, please visit my website, www.Retirewhole.com, where you will be able to email me at any time. I look forward to hearing from you.

APPENDIX

LOVE LETTER LEGACY

Dear family:

I want to make things easier for you, so I have written this letter to provide information that will be necessary for you when the time arises. While this letter is not legally binding, it should be kept with legal documents. I hope you find this helpful.

When I am gone, I hope you will learn from my experiences:

I firmly believe that the most important things in life are:

This is the most important thing to me that I have ever done in my life:

It is my hope that you will use your inheritance from me to accomplish these goals in your life:

Please remember me this way:

These are the people I would like to be pallbearers at my funeral:

I would prefer a traditional funeral _____ or I would prefer a celebration of life_____.

I would like this person or these people to speak at my funeral/celebration of life:

Other information that you feel is important for people to know about you:

Words of wisdom for specific individuals:

Important records and locations
Attorney
Insurance agent
Accountant
Mortgage holder
Financial planner
Others

Income
Company name (if working)
Contact at company
Benefits
Business ownership (if applicable)

If retired

Pension income

Company

Contact

Annuity income

Company

Contact

Veteran benefits

Description of military service

Years of service

Contact at VA

Assets

Account numbers

Titles of accounts

Custodian contact number

Investments

Contact

Phone number

Liabilities

Contact

Phone number

Location of related documents

Credit cards

Companies

Card number

Do you have frequent flyer miles or hotel points accumulated?

In the event of my death
Funeral parlor:
Prepaid cemetery plot:
I am an organ donor.
I do___ I do not____ want to be cremated.
I do___I do not ____ want my body donated to science.

Special requests
Family history:

NON-FINANCIAL RETIREMENT PLAN
Hobbies/interests:

List current hobbies:

List potential hobbies:

What prohibited you from developing potential hobbies?

What do you see as prohibiting factors now?

What needs to be done to overcome these factors?

<u>Volunteer work</u>
List current volunteer work:

List potential volunteer work:

Is there a way to incorporate some of your talents/hobbies into volunteer work?

List part-time employment that you have thought of as being fun:

List part-time employment that you can incorporate into one of your hobbies:
For example, golf pro, piano teacher, personal trainer, tutor.

Marriage tune-up
Go see a counselor for preventive maintenance.
Go on at least one actual date per week.
Spend some time apart each day even if it is only an hour or two.

Evaluate family situations
Do you want to spend more or less time with your grandkids?

Set some specific goals, and establish specific boundaries if necessary.

Fill out the "Love Letter Legacy" section previously mentioned.

Health
Set some specific health goals. Make them small and achievable. Reward yourself periodically for hitting your goals.

Goals:
1.
2.
3.

Rewards:
1.
2.
3.

OTHER HELPFUL WEBSITES:

www.retirewhole.com
www.justserve.org
www.nextavenue.org

ABOUT THE AUTHOR

RYAN S. KIDD has worked as a financial advisor for the past ten years, specializing in the financial aspects of retirement. Additionally Ryan has a master's degree in counseling that helps him better understand the non-financial issues that retirees face.

Throughout his career, Kidd has encountered many people who eventually realize that their concerns about the future extend beyond money to other aspects of retirement, such as grandkids, excess free time, and spending more time with a spouse. *The Art of Retiring Whole* addresses these issues.

REFERENCES

1. Knickman JR, Snell EK. The 2030 Problem: Caring for Aging Baby Boomers. *Health Serv Res.* 2002;37(4):849-884.

2. National Sleep Foundation. National Sleep Foundation Recommends New Sleep Times. Available at: https:// sleepfoundation.org/media-canter/press-release/ nationsl-sleep-foundation-recommends-new -sleep-times. Accessed March 2016.

3. Peri C. Coping With Excessive Sleepiness: 10 Things to Hate About Sleep Loss. *WebMD.* Available at: http://www. wemd.com/sleep-disorddrs/ecessive-sleepiness-10/10-results-sleep-loss. Accessed: March 2016.

4. Kerse N, et al. Home-Based Activity Program for Older People With Depressive Symptoms: DeLITTE-A Randomized Controlled Trial. *Ann Fam Med.* 2010;8(3): 214-223.

5. Paquet C, St-Arnaud-McKenzie D, Ma Z, Kergoat MJ, Ferland G, Dube L. More than just not being alone: the number, nature, and complementarity of meat-time social interactions influence food intake in hospitalized elderly patients. *Gerontologist.* 2008;48(5):603-611.

6. Piper R. 10 Life Changing Tips Inspired by B.K.S. Iyengar. Available at: http://www.mindbodygreen.com/0-5315/ 10-Life-Changiong-Tips-Inspired-By-BKS-Iyengar.html. Accessed: March 2016.

7. Vyain S, ScaramuzzoG, Cody-Rydzewski S, et al. Chapter 13:Aging and the Elderly. In: Introduction to Sociology-1st Canadian Edition. 2013. Wiliam Little, Canada.

8. Caplan M. The Basics of Personal Training for Seniors. American College of Sports Medicine. January 2014. Available at: http://certification.acsm.org/blog/2014/ january/the-basics-of-personal-training-for-seniors. Accessed: March 2016.

9. Computer Use and Exercise Combo May Reduce the Odds of Having Memory Loss, Mayo Clinic Finds. Mayo Clinic Journal. 2012. Available at: http://newsnetwork. mayoclinic.org/discussion/computer-use-and-exercise-combo-may-reduce-the-odds-of-having-memory-loss-mayo-clinic-finds/. -: March 2016.

10. Franklin MB. Retirement planning is now a family affair. Investment News. 2013. Available at: http://www.agewave. com/media_files/11%2024%2013%20InvestmentNews_ Retirement%20planning%20is%20now%20a%20 family%20affair.pdf. Accessed: March 2016.